P9-CKB-844

WE
GATHER
TOGETHER

ALSO BY DENISE KIERNAN

The Girls of Atomic City:
The Untold Story of the Women Who Helped Win World War II

The Last Castle:
The Epic Story of Love, Loss, and American Royalty
in the Nation's Largest Home

WE
GATHER
TOGETHER

⟨※⟩

A NATION DIVIDED,
A PRESIDENT IN TURMOIL,
AND A HISTORIC CAMPAIGN
TO EMBRACE GRATITUDE
AND GRACE

⟨※⟩

DENISE KIERNAN

DUTTON

DUTTON

An imprint of Penguin Random House LLC
penguinrandomhouse.com

Copyright © 2020 by Denise Kiernan
Penguin supports copyright. Copyright fuels creativity, encourages diverse voices, promotes free speech, and creates a vibrant culture. Thank you for buying an authorized edition of this book and for complying with copyright laws by not reproducing, scanning, or distributing any part of it in any form without permission. You are supporting writers and allowing Penguin to continue to publish books for every reader.

DUTTON and the D colophon are registered trademarks of
Penguin Random House LLC.

LIBRARY OF CONGRESS CATALOGING-IN-PUBLICATION DATA

Names: Kiernan, Denise, author.
Title: We gather together: a nation divided, a president in turmoil, and a historic campaign to embrace gratitude and grace
Description: New York: Dutton, 2020. | Includes bibliographical references and index.
Identifiers: LCCN 2020030538 (print) | LCCN 2020030539 (ebook) | ISBN 9780593183250 (hardcover) | ISBN 9780593183267 (ebook)
Subjects: LCSH: Hale, Sarah Josepha Buell, 1788–1879. | Thanksgiving Day—History. | Holidays—United States—History. | Women authors, American—Biography. | United States—History—Civil War, 1861–1865—Social aspects.
Classification: LCC GT4975 .K52 2020 (print) | LCC GT4975 (ebook) | DDC 394.2649—dc23
LC record available at https://lccn.loc.gov/2020030538
LC ebook record available at https://lccn.loc.gov/2020030539
p.   cm.

Printed in the United States of America
1   3   5   7   9   10   8   6   4   2

While the author has made every effort to provide accurate telephone numbers, internet addresses, and other contact information at the time of publication, neither the publisher nor the author assumes any responsibility for errors or for changes that occur after publication. Further, the publisher does not have any control over and does not assume any responsibility for author or third-party websites or their content.

For Joe

CONTENTS

PART III. A REVOLUTION OF GRACE

KEYSTONE STATE,
ETERNAL CITY

Waiting at the depot, the team of horses began approaching its iron counterpart. After the engineers had uncoupled the four passenger cars from the steam engine, the beasts went to work hauling them off one set of tracks and onto another, and adding one more car to the short train for the remainder of the journey. Once off in their new direction, the five cars would follow the tracks stretching out before them to their final destination and the thousands who anxiously awaited them there.

The train's journey had begun that morning in Washington, DC, its passengers bound farther north. One passenger descended there at the Calvert Street Station in Baltimore, waiting for the equine railroad workers to move his car onto the freight line of the Northern Central Railroad. He was headed to western Pennsylvania, where the cheering crowds that awaited him would stand in stark contrast to the somber occasion that was the reason for his trip. But these were

somber times. These were the days when the most enthusiastic of voices were carried on the same winds that just
months earlier were rife with the smell of gunpowder, teeming with cries of anguish, not joy, rising above the blood-
soaked land. These were times that mingled suffering with
satisfaction, gains with gut-wrenching setbacks. The passenger waited for the next leg of the journey, coffins stacked on
the platform around him. This was war.

Some 130 miles to the east of his Keystone State destination stood the city where this young country had begun not
yet ninety years earlier. In that city a galvanizing idea, one of
independence from tyranny, had united citizens of different
walks and varying ideals. Representatives had argued, yes,
differed but ultimately had come together. United.

That city was now a bustling hub of commerce, and there
an editor waited, an editor whose father had fought in that
revolution decades earlier, an editor who now watched what
her father had fought for slipping away. That editor had
come to wield more influence than she could ever have imagined, unearthing voices previously unheard, battling for that
which she valued. Yet that influence was still not enough to
achieve the goal she had been striving toward for much of
her adult life. She needed someone of greater importance,
someone with a more powerful reach and voice. Someone on
a train headed to her state to use that very voice.

She had been waiting for more than thirty years to see
her idea, her heartfelt desire, come to fruition. Like so many
people published before and during her time, she had had
ideas ignored and cast aside, views discounted, opportunities
limited. She was a woman who had risen to the top of a

profession she had never expected to have, one that she had crafted more out of need than of want. But she had always risen to the occasion.

He was a man of contentious proclamations. He was not their first choice to speak that day. He knew that. He, too, would rise to the occasion.

A woman and a man. A media mogul and the most powerful politician in the land. Both hailed from much humbler beginnings; she on a farm, he in a fabled log cabin, countrysides far from the East Coast hubs that they each now called home.

He now wielded power in the halls of the nation's capital; she now wielded a pen in the offices of the country's publishing mecca.

She was far from perfect, as was he. But they were somehow perfectly suited to this occasion, seeking unity in different ways, ways neither had thought might align. Not under these circumstances, not in these divisive times.

Their paths had never crossed, yet in one week, their fates would intertwine. Her intention would meet his execution, her will finding his willingness.

A country torn apart might one day—or for just one day—seek to come together.

The table was set.

The train pulled away from the station.

—❦—

Origin stories are at once enticingly satisfying and perilously fraught with missteps and minefields.

Take the mythic origin story of the city of Rome, Italy, for example. To put it ever so briefly: The god Mars impregnates a Vestal Virgin named Rhea Silvia, whose father's reign over the kingdom of Alba Longa has been usurped by his own brother. Rhea gives birth to twin boys, and her power-hungry uncle—the one who snatched the throne from Rhea's father—orders the babies drowned in the Tiber River in order to prevent them from ever making any claim to the throne of Alba Longa, considered by legend to be the oldest city in Latium. After the would-be assassins set the infants adrift on the river, rather than succumbing to those swirling, ancient Italian waters, the twins alight safely ashore, plopped beneath a fig tree. There, they are suckled by a she-wolf and fed by a woodpecker. The two boys, Romulus and Remus, grow up, rally their forces, and take back Alba Longa from their scheming, murderous great-uncle.

Then, naturally yet somewhat ironically, the grown brothers themselves fight for power—not at all unlike their grandfather and great-uncle. Romulus slays his brother, Remus; a magnificent new city is built upon the Capitoline Hill and named Rome, in honor of Romulus. Then, around 600 BCE, Rome, her power vastly strengthened, destroys Alba Longa—the very kingdom from which the twins' mother hailed.

It is a messy story, and one would be hard-pressed to find an ounce of truth in it. But a compelling origin story, whether mythical or factual, and despite any enduring appeal, lives and thrives as much in the many questions it raises as it does in any answers it seeks to offer. And in that ongoing existence, history is continually evolving.

New insights and understanding gleaned from scientific

fact, painstakingly researched annals, and more, give history a limited shelf life. It happens year after year, generation after generation. Archaeological digs. Uncovered manuscripts. Technological advancements. Stories long set in the canon of a culture, yet defined in their scope by the information initially available, are illuminated, enhanced, and revealed in greater, ideally more comprehensive detail—much like Michelangelo releasing David from the marble that had entrapped him.

Now, Rome has offered much to the world's culture factually, mythically, artistically, and at times violently, ever since those twins Romulus and Remus were weaned from the she-wolf. There is one thing Rome has not, however, easily provided the world or its citizens—and that is easy access to cranberries.

I found this out firsthand when I was in my early thirties. As an American, celebrating Thanksgiving abroad can be a joyous and at times hilariously frustrating experience. I was living in Rome for the second time in my life—my first sojourn there coming right after college when I found myself unable to leave, sucked into the sometimes *dolce*, often frustrating, but ultimately beguiling *vita* of the expat. This time, I had returned on purpose, and was freelancing. Many of my Roman and American friends were still living there, and many were familiar with the concept of American Thanksgiving. Now, while the city is charmingly notorious for shutting down in the middle of the day for siesta, it does not shut down for American holidays. And so celebrating the feast day that Italians refer to as the *giorno del ringraziamento*— literally "day of thanks"—often results in making do with dishes like *salsa di mirtilli* (blueberry sauce) or substituting *ribes* (currants) for that indispensable Thanksgiving staple, cranberries. The cranberry is called *mirtillo rosso americano* in Italian, which means "red American blueberry." They were, when I lived abroad in the early aughts, wickedly difficult to get your hands on in the Eternal City.

If there is Black Friday in America, there is Cranberry November in Rome. Throughout the city, expat Americans outmaneuver one another with the ferocity of razor-elbowed shoppers prowling big-box stores and vying for the last available must-have du jour. They desperately seek out and barter for even the perma-ridged, sugar-soaked, elusive cans of premade cranberry sauce, the kind that exits its container with a *pffft* and a plop and sits on your plate, jiggling, a little crimson tube of jellied nostalgia. Thank God for connections at the United Nations' Food and Agriculture Administration, and its expat-friendly commissary. *Ocean Spray!* My kingdom for some bog-raked Ocean Spray!

Rome was not the first city beyond United States borders where I attempted to celebrate an American Thanksgiving. Years earlier, in fact, I had joined several friends in descending upon the apartment and hospitality of a French friend living in Paris. After a long yet ultimately successful quest for a turkey—a whole one that had had *most* of its feathers removed—we transported what I was sure was one of the smallest birds I had ever seen back to the flat. There we realized that the bird was actually big compared to the French oven expected to fully contain it. The oven door would not shut. Cooking turkey is already a marathon event. It takes a lot longer to accomplish when a good 30 percent of the heat is escaping via an open oven door. We waited. We laughed. We—eventually—ate. We were thankful to be among friends. We were thankful not to get food poisoning.

Money was tight. I had decided not to travel home for the holidays that year, which was not particularly unusual. In fact, I had spent more than a few Thanksgivings at the homes of others. I had traditions I held dear that had nothing to do with my own family, but rather my adopted ones.

And yet whether I was scouring the streets of Rome for cranberries and nutmeg or arguing with the monsieur behind the counter of a French *boucherie* about how a turkey was supposed to be prepared for roasting, I often wondered what had brought me to this desperate state and why I cared. Why do Americans cling so fervently to this holiday? Why was I doing this? Why do so many of us do this every year, no matter our religion, ethnic background, feelings for our relatives, or discomfort with the holiday's own troubling origin stories—many of which have been revealed to be myth?

Thanksgiving weekend has served as an emotional touchstone for me in many ways, and not always a pleasant one. Even today, the long weekend brings up a variety of trying memories: A death in the family. A particularly painful breakup I never saw coming (and as a romantic pessimist, I almost *always* saw them coming). Screaming matches. And, rest her soul, my mother's lackluster stuffing.

Add to this cornucopia of melancholy the fact that I have long known—as so many of us have—that the holiday can be even more painful for Indigenous peoples, many of whom mark the event as a day of mourning year after year to broaden the understanding of how the holiday has evolved in North America.

But I'm getting ahead of myself.

That Thanksgiving weekend that had seen me essentially kicked to the airport curb by a newly minted ex, a dear friend picked me up and took me home. I cried into my yams but was happy being with people who cared for even the messiest version of me.

Yes, other Thanksgivings had seen deaths in the family— but there had been celebrations and births, too. I soon learned to make my own selection of stuffings, and one year I even helped assemble that unholiest of culinary orgies, a turducken: a turkey stuffed with a duck, stuffed with . . . you get the picture. It's like a poultry nesting doll with gravy.

I love celebrating Thanksgiving. There is something about knowing that one weekend a year, things will slow down a bit. I will not have to buy presents or send cards, and there is no particular *religious* practice associated with this holiday that would make me or anyone else feel uncomfortable. It is a time for food and friends. It is a time to say, above all else, things may be kind of a disaster right now, but thank you. I'm grateful to be here, whatever "here" happens to be offering right now.

From the *mirtilli* to the mashed potatoes, my version of Thanksgiving—like that of so many other individuals—has evolved over time. I want to feel good about Thanksgiving. But it has also begun to feel as though it is on the cusp of another evolution, in what we know of it and how we celebrate it now.

Years ago, I began looking into the stories behind both "little-*t*" thanksgivings and the American "big-*T*" Thanksgiving, and that meant exploring more than just decades of menus and historical whitewashing. There is a lot of history there. The origins of the day were rooted in hundreds, even thousands, of years teeming with times of loss and difficulty. Yet thanksgivings, both secular and religious, along with harvest festivals, days of fasting, and the conflation of all of the above, have all had at least one thing in common: gratitude.

Thanksgivings long predate the existence or even conceptualization of the United States. Civilizations of Indigenous peoples were offering thanks in their way tens of thousands of years before Romulus and Remus were even a twinkle in Mars's eye. And in this, humankind's seeking of gratitude and grace—whether or not it is sought with hands clasped at the table—remains relevant, even crucial, especially in the times that try our souls most.

In the midst of strife and suffering, when violence and hatred seem to dominate the news of the day, finding blessings, however big or small, can feel like an insurmountable, even Pollyanna, task. When we're besieged by gloom and feeling alienated and frustrated, hopelessness and anger seem the only logical stances from which to formulate action. We kick into emotional survival mode. But it is precisely in those moments that seeking reasons to be grateful is most important and, as modern neuroscientific evidence continues to support, even healing and curative. Giving thanks when there seems little to be thankful for can offer moments of unity amid division, elicit empathy rather than foster estrangement, and perhaps promote a moment's peace. Toiling to uncover that little speck of gold amid so much emotional dross, we commit to coming together even when we feel forces ripping us apart.

And that appeared to be, at least in part, some of the thinking in 1863 during the American Civil War.

There was, during that contentious time, a controversial president at the helm of a nation that had never been more divided. There was, too, a member of the press on a very particular mission. That powerful member of the media had a mind for years to recommit the country to a unifying celebration of giving thanks, one that might cement what had been for generations—eons, really—a tradition interpreted in many different ways.

This would not be, of course, the final say on the idea of thanksgiving, on these shores or beyond them. It was not about to whom this celebration would belong, beyond that it might be celebrated the same time each year in the same country. In truth, it was less about the proposed holiday than what it might stand for. Could stand for. And might continually strive to evolve into, once the smoke had cleared the battlefield and the plates had cleared the tables.

Over time, we in these oh so young United States have tweaked, teased, reinvented, and expanded both the practice of thanksgiving and the holiday itself to suit our culture, our circumstances, and our traditions, and often to cater to forces whose aims might not have been the noblest—or that were, at the very least, of questionable intent. Just as the myths of Romulus and Remus eventually gave way to the very true stories of Etruscans and Caesars, then so, too, can outdated histories gain a broadened perspective when a culture and a people grow in understanding and, ideally, empathy for those who might wish to gather together to give thanks with us.

And so to see how thanks can arise out of suffering and how the practice of giving thanks might still yet manage to imbue a holiday rife with its own suffering and injustices, it is useful and instructive to first look to the past before bringing this practice forward.

I do not start at "the beginning" of what it means to give thanks, or to create rites and feast days surrounding the practice of gratitude. That is the beginning of time. As a woman and a journalist seeking to reframe the timeless concept of gratitude within the very time-restricted holiday of Thanksgiving in the United States, I looked to another woman and journalist: that same dogged member of the media who pushed presidents to create a national day of thanks but, because of her gender, would never be permitted to cast a vote in the elections of her homeland. Still, she sought to be heard. A writer whose work was unlikely to be widely read. Someone who knew loss. A person who had endured hardship. Through it all, though the world in which she lived either did not want to hear what she thought or gave her very prescribed ways in which she could communicate those thoughts, she carved out a voice. She could not vote for the presidents of her day, but her impact on those leaders and the country they served would outlast all of their lives. She was a cultural bridge of sorts, from one president to the next, and from one version of the country to the next. She was anachronistic in her own way, stubbornly existing in one era, striving in some ways to reach the next, yet not quite fully standing in either. She resisted the limits placed on her by that which had come before and the established expectations of that which was to come. She strove, against many odds, to make things her own.

Thanksgiving is a concept going back thousands of years. Since becoming a national holiday in the United States, it has grown and changed, added some traditions and shirked others. It will continue to do so. In the spirit of one American's time, in the spirit of that one American's enthusiastic fight to raise her voice and elevate those of others, the table is set for change once more. Maybe it is time to make the case for "little-*t*" thanksgiving, one that might embody the best of who we are, one that would argue again for coming together respectfully, when it seems difficult or impossible to do so. Traditions, holidays, practices, celebrations, and more should embody—to quote that very president most closely associated with the annual feast—the "better angels of our nature."

Gratitude, in any case, is not about a holiday; it is about a state of mind. Now, as ever, we need a way to say thanks. We have seen trying times. They have challenged and revealed us. They will again and again.

So before we go any further, we must first take a look back.

I

TIMELESS THANKS

He is a wise man who does not grieve for the things which he has not, but rejoices for those which he has.

—EPICTETUS

CHAPTER 1

AND THUS COMMENCED . . .

S ummer began to slowly yield to autumn with an earlier dip of the sun over the New Hampshire horizon and a dip of the mercury on the thermometer. It was a time for harvest, good or bad, one that might meet or fall short of expectations, needs, and wants. No matter that season's yield, this woman would, along with all the others in her place and time, take a moment, or even a day, to stop and give thanks.

She expected that the state's governor would, as was custom by this point in time, proclaim when this somewhat annual, yet always changeable, celebration and day of reflection would take place. Despite a life that had brought her so much upheaval of late, and no matter her precarious financial situation, and with all of her recent and still deeply resonating loss, she welcomed the opportunity to find something, anything, for which to be grateful.

With her options severely limited and five young mouths

to feed, the woman would do what she had always done. The one thing that brought her some measure of joy.

She was tired.

It was late.

There was a hungry baby at her breast.

Because of her gender she had little standing, but always a foundation on which she was willing to bravely stand. Her options were few. But she had a pen and a purpose and something to say.

And so as she had so many times before, Sarah Josepha Hale sat down to write.

Writing was never a vocation that a young Sarah had actively sought, despite her love of the written word and her rabid consumption of books—one of the few indulgences women were allowed. Even if writing had long been her goal, it was not the kind of calling encouraged in the young women of her time. No, she needed work and she needed money. Life thus far may not have provided her much in the way of opportunity, but it had prepared her well to make do and get by.

Sarah Josepha Buell had spent her childhood in the late 1700s on a farm just outside of Newport, New Hampshire, which sat near the Sugar River. The year she was born, 1788, the recently liberated colonies had yet to elect their first president. Farm life instilled in young Sarah, as it did in many rural folk, a work ethic necessary for survival, especially in the harsh climate of the states' northern reaches. For Sarah, this drive also likely stemmed from witnessing as a child the struggles endured by her father, Gordon Buell, a

Revolutionary War veteran who had fought under General Horatio Gates. Although her father survived those battles, he had returned to his family injured, with the use of his legs badly compromised. This in turn badly compromised his ability to run a farm. So he had long relied on his sons, Sarah's brothers, Horatio and Charles, to help him.

Sarah also had a younger sister, Martha, named for their mother, and the young women helped their mother run the house. As for her two older brothers, Charles soon set out to sea and Horatio, whom they called "Race," was left on his own to help Gordon Buell with the manual labor the family's farm required.

Given that Martha Buell had fed her children's minds in the best way she knew how—with ample helpings of books— it wouldn't be a surprise that Race's aspirations were to pursue college and law, not farming and agriculture. For young women not attending school, reading strongly shaped Sarah's early years as well.

"Next to the Bible and *Pilgrim's Progress*," she later wrote, "my earliest reading was Milton, Johnson, Pope, Cowper, and a part of Shakespeare." But the book that made the biggest impression on her, at a mere seven years of age, was *The Mysteries of Udolpho*, by Ann Radcliffe. "Of all the books I saw," Sarah added, "few were written by Americans and none by *women*. But here was a work, the most fascinating I had ever read, always excepting *Pilgrim's Progress*, written by a *woman*. How happy it made me!"

And so Sarah was educated, primarily in the only way a young woman could be at that time—through books and conversation, yes, but also by intellectually piggybacking on the educations of the males in her life, like her brother Race. Race thought it unfair his sister was denied a college education, and what he learned at school, he generously shared with Sarah, including philosophy and Latin. Between her mother's example and her brother's encouragement, Sarah's fertile mind and growing passion for reading and writing had well prepared her for some sort of work outside the home. That is, if she could get it.

Race—with the benefit of traditional schooling—had been preparing to attend Dartmouth, with the intention of becoming a lawyer. Though his attendance there took him away from the Buell household and therefore placed added pressure on Sarah and her younger sister, Race's visits home to see his family offered Sarah even more advanced opportunities to continue her hand-me-down education.

However, Race's visits home didn't give him enough time to provide the assistance Gordon Buell needed in order to keep the farm running, and so it became clear to Sarah's father that things had to change. He decided he had to seek other, less physically taxing options for work. With his energies waning and his resources drying up, he moved his wife and two daughters into town, where he decided to try his hand as an innkeeper. Gordon Buell opened the doors of the Rising Sun Inn on Newport's main thoroughfare in 1810. Sarah was twenty-two years old.

Now living in the town of Newport, Sarah, with her mind full of books and a thorough if secondhand education at her disposal, sought work as a teacher. This occupation was still considered primarily a job for men who had had the benefit of formal schooling, but exceptions were sometimes made if the need in the community was there. The nearby town of Guild had just such a need, and Sarah began teaching there to earn money for her family. There she was able to share what she had learned and observe the lives of the youngsters in her care. As she did—as she would continue to do—she made note of what she saw in her tiny schoolhouse day to day, and those experiences would inform her writing for years to come.

Race was away at school, Gordon Buell had his inn, and Sarah had her job. Things in Newport were seeming settled, if challenging. The family had not heard from Sarah's older brother, Charles, for some time, long enough that he was presumed lost at sea. They all felt Race's absence. And now, not long after the Rising Sun Inn opened, on November 25, 1811, the Buell family encountered yet another loss. On that day, Sarah's sister, Martha, died of consumption, or tuberculosis. Adding to the family's grief, Sarah's mother passed away shortly thereafter. Now only Sarah and her father remained at home. Without his wife's efforts and support, and with Sarah now occupied with her teaching responsibilities, Gordon Buell was finding it increasingly difficult to maintain the inn.

Living in town also meant that Sarah was interacting with more people and passers-through. And though 1811 had brought loss and turmoil to the household, it also brought something new and exciting to Sarah's life, in the form of a lawyer named David Hale. Taverns were indispensable locales in a small town: a place to meet; get food, drink, or lodging; find out the latest news. David had come to Newport to open his own law office and shortly after his arrival, the newcomer stopped into the Rising Sun Inn. And there he met Sarah.

David was older than she, but the pair were impeccably well suited to each other. And though Sarah's father eventually sold the inn, it was there that the pair married on October 23, 1814. Sarah was a day shy of her twenty-sixth birthday. The two moved into a lovely two-story white-painted wooden house on the town's main street. It had plenty of windows and ample light, and sat across from several small streams that ran through the center of town and created small islets that residents would hop and traverse to get from one side to the other. The pair filled their house with those very objects they both cherished most: books.

Sarah delighted in the evenings she and David spent sitting together to read and discuss the books that filled their shelves. They even devised a nightly program of study, lending goals and purpose to their favorite pastime. From eight in the evening until ten, the couple studied topics like French and botany. In some ways, David had taken up where Race had left off, sharing the benefits of his formal education with Sarah. "In all our mental pursuits," she later wrote, "it seemed the aim of Mr. Hale to enlighten my reason, strengthen my judgement, and give me confidence in my own powers of mind, which he estimated much higher than I did." And with David's encouragement, Sarah had also begun to dedicate more time to her writing. Her observations and notes evolved into poems and short stories. She did not, she would later say, want her personal life in the pages of her works. Yet her personal beliefs, her views, and her passions often infused her characters.

The couple quickly grew their family. While pregnant with her third child, Sarah came down with tuberculosis, and it was feared she and the unborn child would die, victims of a disease that had already struck Sarah's own family. David refused to accept this. Against doctor's orders, he took his wife on a tour of New Hampshire. It was late autumn and brisk. David had heard that fresh air was healing and that "frost grapes"—wild grapes exposed to the first frost while still on the vine—were curative. The pair returned home and, somewhat miraculously, Sarah regained her strength and gave birth to a healthy baby. A fourth followed soon after. And since they had seemed to work, Sarah would continue to eat grapes for the rest of her days.

Sarah was now busy taking care of the home and, as her mother had for her, educating her children. David was occupied with his practice and active in the Newport community, and had been elected Worshipful Master of the Corinthian Lodge of the Masons. Sarah's father, Gordon, had died just five years after his daughter married, so this was Sarah's family now, save for visits from her brother Race, who, like her husband, was now a lawyer. Growing in experience if not in confidence, Sarah began to take on larger and larger writing projects, with David encouraging her to submit those pieces to the local newspapers or other outlets that might publish them. Sarah's experiences as a teacher, the settings and rhythms of life in New England, as well as her cherished role as a mother—which she considered her first vocation—informed and inspired some of her earliest writing. And her children comprised her earliest audience. When it was time to put her four youngsters to sleep, Sarah would share her own poetry with them.

"Good night," she'd say.

*Good night—and peace be
with you—
Peace, that gentlest parting
strain;
Soft it falls like dew on
blossoms,
Cherishing within our bosoms,
Kind desires to meet again:
Good night—Good night.*

*Good night—Good night—
but not forever,
Hope can see the morning rise,
Many a pleasant scene before
us,*

*As though angels hovered o'er
us,
Bearing blessings from the
skies:
Good night—Good night.*

*Good night—Good night—oh,
softly breathe it!
'Tis a prayer for those we love;
Peace to-night and joy
to-morrow,
For our God, who shields the
sparrow,
Hears us in his courts above:
Good night—Good night.*

In 1822, at the age of thirty-three, Sarah was expecting her fifth child. What she was not expecting, not so early into their marriage, not with a child weeks away from being born, was that David would take ill. It was late September, the air was turning cold, and David was returning home from visiting a client. Wintry weather was unexpected on this, an early fall day, but it arrived nonetheless and David found himself caught in it. At first, he was struck by a cold, but then his symptoms advanced. David soon succumbed to pneumonia, an illness Sir William Osler, the father of modern medicine, would later dub "the most fatal of all acute diseases." And so it was. David did not recover.

Sarah had not yet been married ten years. The couple's fifth child, William, entered the world just two weeks after his father's departure from it. Sarah had donned her mourning black for David's burial at Pine Hill Cemetery in Newport, and she would wear it the rest of her days.

Sarah Josepha Hale was now a thirty-four-year-old widowed mother of five. She had never earned enough of a living from her writing to support a family. "Till my husband's death . . . I had never seriously contemplated being an authoress," Sarah later wrote. With a lawyer for a husband, she had not needed to. But as with most paths taken in life, Sarah's was partially forged by necessity. Now, she needed money.

"My husband's business had been large for the country," Sarah wrote later, describing the relative success of a lawyer working outside of a major city such as Boston or New York, "but he had hardly reached the age when men of his profession begin to lay up property and he had spared no indulgence to his family. We had lived in comfort, but I was left poor," she wrote, adding, "for my children I was deeply distressed. I care not that they should inherit wealth, but to be deprived of the advantages of education was to make them 'poor indeed.'"

Sarah's first attempt to rebuild her family's finances was to go into business with David's sister Hannah and open a millinery in town. The local Masons, in the wake of David's sudden death, offered to help set up the pair in a shop of their own. The two women placed an ad in the local newspaper, *Spectator*, to announce their new business and offerings to the residents of Newport: figured gauze, hats for daily wear, silk mourning bonnets, brown cambrics, headdresses, and more. They assured potential customers they offered "the latest and most assured patterns." As for payment, they would happily take currency or even feathers. But there was plenty of competition as well. And Sarah simply did not want to make mourning bonnets. She wanted to write.

Nights proved the most opportune time to get writing done. Her days were packed with work at the shop, as well as caring for her four children and newborn William. But she made the most of the time she could spare, and Sarah's steady commitment to her writing netted her an accumulation of poems that she thought might make a nice collection. Within a year after David's death, in 1823, and again with the fortunate backing of the Masons, Sarah published *The Genius of Oblivion; and Other Original Poems*. The title page described the author simply as "A Lady of New Hampshire." Despite its mediocrity, its publication was a major accomplishment for Sarah. Nevertheless, the book garnered little attention or critical praise. Undeterred, she decided to submit her work to more widely read publications, and almost immediately the *United States Literary Gazette*, the *Atlantic Monthly*, and the *Boston Spectator and Ladies' Album* snapped up her work. In fact, the latter published seventeen of Sarah's poems, two short stories, and a review—in one year alone. She was beginning to get noticed. Several of her poems were also included in a popular gift book, *The Memorial*. Momentum was hers, and she was eventually able to wish her sister-in-law well and leave the millinery behind.

The years of nightly writing soon reaped an even larger reward: Sarah had completed a weighty novel. She sent off the manuscript to one of the country's major publishing hubs at the time, Boston, and into the hands of, as she later wrote, "a stranger." Soon after, she traveled to Boston to meet with the publishers at Bowles & Dearborn. The institution agreed to publish her book, and in 1827 Sarah's first novel, *Northwood; or, A Tale of New England*, would be in print for anyone who might be interested in reading it. That remained to be seen; depending on what a reader brought to her work and believed, Sarah's themes would prove either compelling or repellant.

The two-volume *Northwood* is set in a country divided in experience and views, if not yet officially torn asunder and at war with itself. Part of the saga took place in Sarah's home state of New Hampshire, while the other part was set in the southern United States on a plantation. Her descriptions of life in New England were much more detailed and nuanced, as she had lived her entire life thus far in the state in which that aspect of the story took place. She—via her characters—upheld life and customs in New England. The language and perspectives of the characters reflected, in many ways, the times in which Sarah lived. Views on slavery espoused by the characters in *Northwood* ranged from abolitionist to paternalistic to racist, from an abhorrence of slavery to its tolerance—much akin to the growing debate in the United States. Sarah's decision to write a book presenting in any manner the institution of slavery was practically unheard of in 1827, especially for a woman. (Harriet Beecher Stowe's *Uncle Tom's Cabin* would not be published for another twenty-five years.)

Northwood managed to strike enough of a chord with the public to garner Sarah a bit more attention—and to sell some copies. This came as a relief to its author.

"To those who know me," she would address her readers years later, "it is also known that this was not entered upon to win fame, but a support for my little children. *Northwood* was written literally with my baby in my arms—the 'youngling of the flock,' whose eyes did not open on the world till his father's were closed in death!"

The book's success may not have been overly notable, but it appealed to enough readers that it was published in England as well, under the title *Sidney Romelee: A Tale of New England*.

"The Reader who has suffered, or who is struggling to perform sacred duties," Sarah wrote, "will rejoice that this work not only succeeded, but that the mode of its success proved it was not unworthy of public favor."

After the publication of *Northwood* came reviews of Sarah's work, letters of congratulations, and a job offer. She received the opportunity to edit a brand-new magazine just for women: the *Ladies' Magazine*. The new position, should she accept it, would take her to Boston.

"I had many fears for its success," Sarah wrote almost a decade later. "No publication of the kind had been long sustained; but the adventure promised advantages in educating my children—and I accepted."

It was 1828. The railroads were new and connecting the country in ways never previously conceived. Former presidents John Adams and Thomas Jefferson had died on the very same day, July 4, just two years earlier. Only one signer of the Declaration of Independence, Charles Carroll, still lived. Literate Americans were hungry for print—whether newspapers, magazines, or books. Sarah had reached her fortieth year, and the former teacher and milliner, self-taught poet, and now author would add "editor" to her evolving résumé.

"And thus commenced my literary life . . ."

Other women of the time actively sought publication and achieved success at it, often writing for children. In 1827, Lydia Maria Child was editing and publishing the *Juvenile Miscellany*, a publication to which Sarah herself had also contributed. Women editors were in a position to not only communicate their own views but embolden other women to do the same. By accepting the job at the helm of the *Ladies' Magazine*, Sarah had embarked on an extraordinary journey that would, in many ways, defy the very limitations that she, as a decidedly apolitical individual, never actively sought to change. In the years to come, she would advocate for one overarching cause: education for women. She believed that this was the best way to improve the lives of all women. And now, with a growing audience, she might be able to rally others to do the same.

When Sarah went off to live in Boston, her son David was doing preparatory work in order to enter the United States Military Academy at West Point. Horatio, named for her brother, would live with his namesake in Glen Falls, New York, to further his own education. Her two daughters, Frances Ann and Sarah Josepha, went to live with their uncle Selma, David Hale's brother, in Keene, New Hampshire. Sarah's youngest child, William, would accompany his mother to their new home.

One thing was certain. Among the many campaigns she would wage there in the pages of her magazine, there was another that would obsess her for years.

It was a theme a reader of *Northwood* would already have spotted. The novel had brought Sarah much needed income, much valued expression of her voice, and a new job in a new city. But through the pages of *Northwood* Sarah had also presented more to the world than views on the North and the South, or a country headed for division. She had also proposed an image of what she considered to be a reason for them to come together. In those pages, in 1827, Sarah put forth an idea that would in time consume her personal and professional lives.

"We should love our native land were it a sterile rock; but we love it better when to our cultivation it yields an ample increase; and the farmer, instead of sighing for foreign dainties, looks up to heaven, and depends on his own labors; and when they are crowned with a blessing, he thanks God, as tens of thousands throughout our State are doing this day. Let us join our voices with theirs."

CHAPTER 2

AN EVOLUTION OF GRATITUDE

What Hale described in her first novel—joining voices with others to give thanks—was not completely without precedent, even if it was not a federally mandated practice. And this sort of tradition long predated any transatlantic crossings of the fifteenth and sixteenth centuries. Even more universal was something so timeless that it seemed without origin at all: the concept of gratitude, and coming together to express it as a community.

Grazie.

Merci.

Asante.

Gracias.

Shukran.

Danke.

Arigato.

Wado.

Thank you.

These two words—if referring to the English language, of course—can wield a tremendous amount of power, whether spoken aloud or merely murmured quietly in our own cluttered headspace. When stated, the phrase may often be uttered in appreciation for assistance, caring, or consideration received during hardship. From the act of showing up emotionally for a friend after a loss to the providing of shelter or food to someone with less, and everything in between, giving thanks reminds humans to look at what one *has*, as opposed to what one *lacks*. This can not only bring peace of mind but can also bring people together. The merest sliver of light and hope stands out so much more starkly amid a deluge of gray and suffering. "Let's focus on that bright spot over there," we tell ourselves, "at least for a little while."

Giving thanks can be a perpetual state of mind, a daily practice, or simply an action done on a particular occasion. It is one that has, over thousands of years, made its way into celebrations and sayings, buttressing prayers and proverbs.

"He is a wise man who does not grieve for the things which he has not, but rejoices for those which he has," believed Greek Stoic philosopher Epictetus. And as an old Buddhist proverb states: "'Enough' is a feast."

The value of thanks was no more true in times of antiquity than in any modern-day adaptation of thanksgivings. Hardship and trials, lack and wanting, were inevitably punctuated by merciful moments of relief. Humans learned to— felt compelled to—take time to express thanks for those very moments. These offerings of thanks took many forms and have long been expressed as festivals, rituals, and celebrations, either secular or religious, and often in a melding of these incarnations. The concept of gratitude and thanks is one that permeates cultures, that appears in the nooks and crannies of the planet, and that did so long before our modern languages had the symbols and alphabets to convey that feeling to others.

Let us return again to Rome. Humans here long have given thanks for food harvested, battles won, hardships endured, enemies vanquished. Famed Roman orator Marcus Tullius Cicero rather notably—and perhaps narcissistically—wrote of his own *supplicatio*, or "thanksgiving," which the people of Rome offered to the gods in honor of Cicero's role in exposing a dangerous plot against the Roman Empire.

"And a thanksgiving to the immortal gods for their singular favor has even been decreed in my name," Cicero wrote, "which I have been the first civilian to obtain since the foundation of this city, and has been decreed in these words: *because I had freed the city from fires, citizens from slaughter, Italy from war.*"

Cicero may or may not have been entirely accurate in his claim that he broke the laudatory mold when it came to civilian thanksgivings and his heroic *supplicatio*. But few would have argued with him. What is notable was each was "a" thanksgiving. Singular. A onetime affair. This kind of celebration stood in some contrast to one of the repeatedly observed festivals in Rome, the Cerealia, honoring the goddess of grain and agriculture, Ceres. According to Roman mythology, when Pluto, god of the Underworld, abducted Ceres's daughter, Proserpina, Ceres wreaked havoc on the earth, leaving it barren. After some negotiations between Jupiter and the Fates, an agreement was struck: Proserpina would spend part of the year with Pluto—resulting in cold, barren winter—and the summer with Ceres, resulting in fruitful crops and bountiful harvests. During the festival, white-clad women brandishing torches ran about to represent Ceres's search for her daughter. But in either case, whether for a singular glory of the republic or for the seasonal worship of a goddess, these kinds of thanksgivings were a part of the Roman culture. And Cicero's own thoughts on the concept of gratitude were also well documented.

"There is nothing which I can esteem more highly than the being and appearing grateful," he reportedly said, "for this one virtue is not only the greatest, but is also the parent of all other virtues."

The Romans may have shared numerous ancient thanksgivings and festivals, but then of course so did the Egyptians and the Greeks and many other cultures. There is the Thesmophoria in Greece, which is named in honor of the goddess Demeter (who was also referred to as "Thesmophoros"). The Greek counterpart of Ceres, Demeter had denied the world food in winter as punishment for the god Hades's abduction of her daughter, Persephone. And when Persephone finally returned, so did agriculture, food, abundance—spring. And so there was a festival of thanks. The Mesopotamian festival of Akitu was celebrated by the ancient Babylonians. The Chinese had Chung Ch'ui, and the Hindus held the festival of Pongol. There are examples from all continents, from the Homowo harvest festival celebrated by the Ga-Adangbe people of Ghana to the Celtic festivities surrounding Lughnasa. Most were centered on thanks for the coming harvest and for food, and, in the case of Lughnasa, a coming together, or assembly.

What were observations of thanks and gratitude in concept then became increasingly evidenced in written history. The religious texts of the monotheistic faiths—Judaism, Islam, and Christianity—provide numerous written references to gratitude and thanks. In the Quran's longest book, the Surah Al-Baqarah, we can read, "O ye who believe! Eat of the good things that We have provided for you, and be grateful to Allah, if it is Him ye worship."

Offering prayer in the Jewish faith can fall into three main categories: praise, petition, and lastly—but not leastly—gratitude, or *Hoda'ah*. Mentioned in the Hebrew Bible, or Tanakh, is thanksgiving. As taken from the book of Leviticus: "With the sacrifice of his peace offerings for thanksgiving, he shall present his offering with cakes of leavened bread." Or look to Nehemiah in chapter 12, where we find "And in the dedication of the wall of Jerusalem, they sought the Levites from all their places to bring them to Jerusalem to perform the dedication with joy, and with thanksgivings, and with song, cymbals, psalteries, and with harps."

In Christianity, gratitude and thanksgiving are frequently communicated ideas. The English word *gratitude* has its roots in Medieval Latin. And we are now able to research increasingly early writings for hints about the term *thanksgiving*, including by examining those inscribed in the Codex Sinaiticus—or Sinai Book—which is considered to be the oldest, most *complete* version of the Christian Bible known today. This codex is considered even more complete than the Codex Vaticanus, the centuries-old segment of the Bible that resides at the Vatican in Rome. The Codex Sinaiticus encompasses the Septuagint, or Old Testament, dating back to the Greek Christians, as well as the New Testament. The religious writings were initially committed by hand on vellum; it is estimated that the texts of the Codex Sinaiticus date to sometime in the middle of the fourth century. This makes this version of the Christian Bible more than sixteen hundred years old. Older selected texts that have been found contain only *parts* of the Bible.

One of the more compelling aspects of the Codex Sinaiticus is that not only does it contain handwritten text, but it also offers corrections and edits to prior versions of the very same text. Throughout those edits and changes and tweaks—as one would expect even from any modern-day manuscript—are many passages that emerged from the editing process virtually unscathed. There are nine mentions in the original Codex Sinaiticus of words that translate to English as "thanksgiving," and those mentions have survived the many subsequent editions of the Bible. From Timothy to Colossians, from Corinthians to Philippians, we have a written record of "thanksgiving" from more than sixteen hundred years ago. For example, from 1 Timothy 2:1, we have the words of the first-century evangelist and disciple Paul the apostle: "I exhort therefore, first of all, that supplications, prayers, intercessions, thanksgivings, be made for all men." Also in 1 Timothy 4:4, we read, "For every creature of God is good, and nothing to be thrown away, being received with thanksgiving . . ."

These appearances of the word are, of course, based on translations. In the development of the English language, a word that would eventually come to conjure images of turkeys and stuffing recipe battles and parades and floats and football games has itself been around for centuries—again, with a variety of meanings and interpretations depending on the occasion.

William Tyndale's 1526 English translation of the New Testament contained *thanksgiving*, along with some phrases that have long endured: "eat, drink and be merry" and "salt of the earth." The word *thankesgevynge* is seen in the Book of Common Prayer, the guide for worship for the Anglican Church, which dates to 1549, as well as in the King James Version of the Bible—the most printed book in history—dating to 1611. Thanksgiving practice was familiar in England. In 1588, for example, after England's defeat of the Spanish Armada, Queen Elizabeth I declared a day of thanksgiving, and a special service was held at St. Paul's Cathedral. Many religious thanksgiving services were often associated with not only prayer but—in irony of all digestible ironies—fasting.

The thanksgiving traditions that were found throughout Europe, including those practiced in England and Holland, would eventually travel when populations from those lands crossed the Atlantic and settled into what is now the eastern coast of the United States. What they brought to this continent was nothing new in spirit, but it came packed within their own languages and traditions. More important, those Indigenous peoples the newcomers encountered upon arriving, people who had already been living on the continent for many years, had their own long-standing traditions of giving thanks.

And so varying expressions of thanksgiving occurred with successive waves of arriving Europeans.

When Francisco Vázquez de Coronado left what would one day be called Mexico City and headed north to look for gold, one of his expedition's stops was at Palo Duro Canyon, in what is now known as the Texas Panhandle. In that May of 1541, while enjoying their rest and feeling thankful for their thus-far-successful journey, Coronado proclaimed there should be a celebration. He and his crew of some fifteen hundred fellow travelers reveled in gratitude, eating what food they could gather. Fray Juan de Padilla celebrated a Mass.

A little more than twenty years after that event, in June 1564, the thankful celebrants were not Spanish but rather the French Huguenots, who established Fort Caroline in Florida, along the St. Johns River, near present-day Jacksonville. The settlement gave thanks in a more solemn manner for their survival thus far, a survival that was short-lived: That settlement was gone within a year. King Philip II of Spain, believing the land to rightfully belong under Spanish control, dispatched a fleet, and soon the Huguenots of Fort Caroline were massacred, losing both land and life to the Spaniards.

The following year, on September 8, 1565, Pedro Menéndez de Avilés founded St. Augustine. Menéndez, upon guiding five ships and some eight hundred Spanish settlers ashore to what was then called Spanish La Florida, joined with his fellow travelers in a thanksgiving Mass, followed by a meal to which Menéndez reportedly invited members of the nearby Timucua tribe. The gathering likely dined on salted pork, garbanzo beans, maybe some hard biscuits and red wine—perhaps even a sampling of gopher tortoise.

Farther north on the continent, in what is modern-day Canada, there was a celebration in November 1606. That feast was a meal between the Indigenous peoples and the newly arrived Europeans—namely Frenchman Samuel de Champlain—in the area known as Port Royal. Eating abundantly and safely was key to survival, and the Mi'kmaq had done more than their part in showing the settlers how to ice fish, as well as which berries just happened to be high in vitamin C. That November 1606 fete reportedly featured a performance of *Théâtre de Neptune*, a play by Frenchman Marc Lescarbot featuring the god Neptune as a main character. It is believed by many to be the first European play performed in North America. Perhaps part "thanksgiving," part dinner theater.

The following year, in 1607 (the same year the colony of Jamestown, Virginia, took root), the settlement of Fort St. George along the Kennebec River in what is now the state of Maine was the site of both a harvest feast and a prayer meeting between the Abenaki and English settlers. That short-lived fort and its inhabitants were gone just a year later, and thus known as the lost colony of Popham. Farther south, in Virginia, the colony of Jamestown was still surviving—if barely. In the spring of 1610, after receiving desperately needed food supplies from overseas, and in honor of surviving the famine-wrought winter of 1609, the 60 of 490 colonists who were still living and breathing (many of whom had already resorted to eating their horses, and their deceased neighbors) gave thanks and commemorated eking out another year in their new land.

Some nine years later, in 1619, Captain John Woodlief and the ship *Margaret* arrived in Chesapeake Bay. The vessel proceeded up the James River and on December 4, 1619, stopped at what was known as Berkeley: "the Great Plantation." Captain Woodlief instructed those aboard to pray. "We ordaine that this day of our ships arrival, at the place assigned for plantacon, in the land of Virginia, shall be yearly and perpetually kept holy as a day of Thanksgiving to Almighty God," Woodlief wrote. Roughly one year later, in 1620, the aptly named ship *Supply* also docked at Berkeley Plantation, this time helmed by one Captain William Tracy. The *Supply* brought fifty new residents, and the day was again celebrated—a second "annual" thanksgiving . . . for the time being, at least.

And so there were harvest festivals, and there were thanksgivings for blessings received of whichever god you happened to worship, and there were also thanksgivings for saving republics from a fiery fate, as well as thanksgivings for successful travel and for survival. Soon these rituals and their associated words—these festivals and thanksgivings, secular and religious alike—became intertwined in this new land. "Thanksgivings" began to conflate over time, somewhat organically, and perhaps not surprisingly, over many years. If gratitude was, as Cicero had so eloquently put it, the parent of all other virtues, gratitude's children had developed some very malleable personalities. Gratitude and giving thanks—

on this continent, let alone in the world—was perhaps the most common of human concepts, one that was universally valued but increasingly locally flavored.

By the time Sarah Josepha Hale decided to make an annual, national thanksgiving holiday a mission of hers in the United States, not only had the concept of thanksgiving celebrations long predated the one she envisioned, it also long predated the festivities she herself had grown up with in New England. In the northern reaches of the states there were days of thanksgiving, prayer, and fasting that had preceded the American Revolution. An annual spring fast and an annual thanksgiving at the time of harvest were custom. By the early nineteenth century, there were many homes that celebrated days designated by governors and other community dignitaries as thanksgivings, with a large gathering of friends and a table full of food.

For Hale, now, the thanksgiving she proposed to see practiced across all the states and territories in America would resemble in flavor the kinds that she herself treasured. But what she sought most was to have every American pause to give thanks at the same time each year, across the country. That would be the message she would begin to trumpet in the pages of her magazine and in the letters she would soon write. If nothing else, she was rooted in her present.

She wanted to further that which unified, which called people to gather as one.

Hale would likely have appreciated the words long used by Haudenosaunee, or the Iroquois Confederacy of Five (eventually Six) Nations:

"Now our minds are one" is a repeated refrain taken from

the Haudenosaunee Thanksgiving Address, or *Gano:nyok*. This translates as "words that come before all else." For gratitude shall come before all else. The Six Nations of the Iroquois—the Seneca, Cayuga, Oneida, Onondaga, Mohawk, and Tuscarora—employ this thanksgiving address on many occasions, to express gratitude not just on any one particular day but throughout the year, and they give this thanks not for one particular thing but for all things: Water. Animals. Mother Earth. The moon and the stars. The address offers "greetings to the natural world."

When it came to gratitude, there was no mistaking: It was here long before the Europeans came, and would remain long after. But when it came to what thanksgiving in the new America might be, minds were rarely one. Hale had an idea of how she wanted her particular holiday to look. She made no claims about who did what first. She knew only what it was she wanted the country to do next.

CHAPTER 3

MEDIA MADONNA

Whether or not it was her intention to do so, and though her professed priority was to find a way to support her children and offer them a good education, Hale's actions while in her new post suggest a strong desire to give voice to the campaigns she held dear to her heart.

The working woman's life in the 1830s was one often limited to the home, the seamstress's shop, the milliner's, the laundry, or, if fortunate, the schoolhouse. While no woman or person of color had the right to vote, Hale soon discovered that in the pages of her magazine and at the helm of its content, she did have a voice, and that voice and its opinions would not be stifled. In a day when the loudest voices were those of men, especially via their political power and in the church, Hale used her own pulpit to advance her goals—often in the service of others.

Shortly after her arrival in Boston, Hale learned of the

forestalled Bunker Hill Monument, intended to commemorate the Revolutionary War battle of the same name. Members of the Bunker Hill Monument Association had secured land and raised enough money to see the cornerstone of the monument laid in 1825. But by 1830, it remained unfinished for lack of funding. Hale, the daughter of an injured Revolutionary War veteran, became devoted to seeing the monument completed. With a new audience, she took to her pages and called for support from her readers. She believed in the aggregate power of small. Noting that if each woman living in New England—some nine hundred thousand of them—were to donate just twenty-five cents, the necessary sum would be raised. The response was not what Hale had hoped for, but she remained undeterred.

"Our doubts are traitors," she penned for the editorial page of her new endeavor. "And make us lose the good we oft might win, by fearing to attempt."

Ladies' Magazine was founded by an Episcopal minister, Reverend John Lauris Blake, and Hale was its editor from the get-go. Putnam & Hunt served as the publication's initial printers, and offices were located on Washington Street in Boston, which was fast becoming a hub for booksellers, publishers, and the like. For three dollars per year, the monthly magazine supplied content that Hale insisted had not been printed elsewhere (a common practice then). She also reluctantly agreed to a fashion column and images for the magazine.

Hale published the work of up-and-coming young poets and writers—many of them women—Lydia Huntley Sigourney, Lydia Maria Child, and Sarah Whitman among them. In addition to her editing responsibilities, Hale contributed her own writing to the publication, including editorials, articles, advice, and reviews. In 1830, the magazine published a review of a book of poems by a promising young author. The review called some of the poems "boyish, feeble, and altogether deficient in the common characteristics of poetry," but admitted there was great potential in the fellow, who, though he "appears to be very young, is evidently, a fine genius; but he wants judgment, experience, tact." Nevertheless, the review deemed the unknown to "remind us of no less a poet than Shelley."

Early in 1831, following the review of this young poet's work, Hale's eldest son, David, wrote to her from West Point, where he was now attending the U.S. Military Academy. The poet was in fact a classmate of his.

"I have communicated what you wrote to Mr. Poe," her son David wrote of his classmate Edgar, whom David described as "too mad a poet to like mathematics." And so began Hale's relationship with Edgar Allan Poe.

Whether she was supporting a mad male poet or an uneducated female essayist, Hale was aware of not only the opportunity but also the challenges facing her as a writer with increased exposure and a woman in a position of editorial power.

"Few females are educated for authorship," she later wrote, "and as the obstacles which oppose the entrance of woman on the fields of literature are many and great, it requires, usually, a powerful pressure of outward circumstances to develop and mature her genius.

"It may be truly said of her that
—'Strength is born
In the deep silence of long suffering hearts,
Not amidst joy.'"

Between her editorial work and parenting, time to pen another of her own novels was proving unmanageable, but Hale was eking out hours here and there to work on a new collection of poems. In the face of each day's shifting challenges, she shifted, too, tacking like a nimble skiff when need be, navigating uncharted waters in a sea of new professional and personal obligations and opportunities.

The thriving city of Boston now provided Hale increased visibility and access to those who might see fit to join forces with her on whatever her latest crusade might be. She reached them not only via her readership but also in her rapidly expanding social circle. The petite, ebon-clad powerhouse was attractive and impeccably well spoken, and Hale the journalist became savvy about forming alliances. She threw herself into her new hometown. She attended lectures, reviewing them on occasion for her readers. She started a literary club. As an accomplished seamstress whose magazine offered homemaking tips and information on schooling, in addition to reviews and fashion plates, she spearheaded a sewing circle that often focused its efforts on making clothes for those in need. Through these activities and charitable pursuits, Hale grew her sphere of influence, allowing her to create useful alliances when it was time to rally forces. One such fortuitous friendship was that which she forged with Deborah Taylor, the wife of Father Edward T. Taylor—a Methodist minister known in Boston and well beyond that city's limits as "the sailor's preacher."

Hale was struck by the scores of impoverished individuals, many of them veterans or their widows, she saw struggling on the streets daily. As someone who herself had been left financially struggling when her own husband died, Hale called upon her readers not to turn a blind eye to the situation engulfing them.

Father Taylor had caught the ear of many a sailor returning to shore, and there were more than a thousand ships docked in Boston in those days. Taylor ministered to the destitute, the shipwreck survivors, the widows of men lost at sea, and also the likes of writers Charles Dickens and Walt Whitman, both of whom clamored to hear the salty man of the cloth when they found themselves in Boston. Whitman wrote of Taylor, "I have never heard but one essentially perfect orator."

Having lost her eldest brother, Charles, to the sea, been widowed at a young age, and now having a son, David, seemingly destined for battle in Florida, Hale was perhaps predisposed by personal tragedy to raise awareness about the suffering of returning seafarers and those women and children left behind in the wake of their losses. And so the Seaman's Aid Society was born.

The society served not only returning sailors themselves, but their families. Hale's efforts resulted in the establishment of an associated school, as well. Raising donations of books proved not too difficult a task, and soon the group created the Seaman's Society Library. Hale railed against inadequate pay for returning veterans and sailors, and the rum-soaked boardinghouses in which so many of them had no choice but to reside. She believed that living surrounded by that sort of dilapidation and filth could only negatively affect those who resided there.

She was finding her footing as an advocate, and her words were profoundly convincing. She keenly pointed out the irony in a sailor's responsibility for moving great wealth across oceans but keeping none of it for himself, and that despite this invaluable role in ensuring the prosperity of others, it was "almost certain that his widow and orphans will be left destitute."

Still a champion of education, Hale wrote poems and verses for children that were destined for the nation's schoolhouses. In 1834, she published the *School Song Book* with Allen & Ticknor of Boston, billing herself as "Mrs. Sarah J. Hale, Editor of the Ladies' Magazine, and author of 'Flora's Interpreter,' &c. &c." Included in that text was a poem believed to have been inspired by her early days teaching in Guild, New Hampshire, when she observed a lamb following one of her students to school. That poem, "Mary's Lamb," would achieve lasting popularity, recited by countless children who remembered it into their adulthood.

Mary had a little lamb,
Its fleece was white as snow,
And every where that Mary
*   went*

The lamb was sure to go:
It followed her to school one
*   day,*
That was against the rule;

It made the children laugh
  and play
To see a lamb at school.

And so the Teacher turned
  him out,
But still he lingered near,
And waited patiently about,
Till Mary did appear:
And then he ran to her, and
  laid
His head upon her arm,
As if he said, "I'm not afraid,

You'll save me from all harm."

"What makes the lamb love
  Mary so?"
The little children cry—
"O Mary loves the lamb, you
  know,"
The Teacher did reply:
"And you each gentle animal
In confidence may bind,
And make them follow at your
  call,
If you are always kind."

The poem had been included in another collection published several years earlier, titled *Poems for Our Children*, as
well as in Lydia Maria Child's *Juvenile Miscellany*. As not
just an editor but also an abolitionist and author, Child was
embroiled in her own professional struggles. Her novel *Hobomok*, in which a Puritan woman marries a Native American man, Hobomok, gained Child notice, but also some
measure of scandal. At this point in history, the federal government was forcibly and violently removing Native peoples
from their eastern lands to points west on the Trail of Tears.

Sympathetic to the plight of Native Americans as well as
enslaved peoples, Child didn't shy away from sharing her
views. She had also recently published *An Appeal in Favor
of That Class of Americans Called Africans*, in which she
called for the immediate emancipation of all enslaved persons with no compensation to the slaveholders. Subscribers
to her children's magazine began to drop. But those kinds of

consequences did not deter her from speaking her mind in an age that both Hale and she knew was far from welcoming to Women with Opinions.

"When I published my first book," Child wrote, "I was gravely warned by some of my female acquaintances that no woman could expect to be regarded as a *lady* after she had written a book."

Hale—by now part owner of *Ladies' Magazine*—found her own subscriptions falling as well, if not for the same reasons as Child. Once Hale had her own stake in the magazine, she had dropped the publication's popular fashion illustrations (of which she was never a fan), which may have impacted the magazine's subscription income. She was struggling. And yet when Child resigned as editor of the *Juvenile Miscellany*, Hale took over that, too, adding even more burden to her already weighty responsibilities. She renamed *Ladies' Magazine* the *American Ladies' Magazine* (to distinguish it from a similarly named publication in England), but keeping the publication afloat was trying her energies as well as her finances. By 1835, subscriptions in arrears were more than $400 (nearly $12,000 in 2020 dollars). Hale had been approached to contribute significantly to yet another magazine, but she wanted to hold on to all she had worked to build in Boston. Boston had become home to her and her youngest son, William. David, her oldest, was indeed off to fight in the Second Seminole War. (This would become the longest war of removal fought by the United States, resulting in the forcible relocation of approximately three thousand members of the Seminole Nation.) Still,

Hale needed to find a solution: a way to maintain and even to build on what she had accomplished thus far and, most important, to be able to continue to support herself and her children.

The media maverick was about to become involved in a merger.

We are confident our readers will not regret the change, when they learn that Mrs. S. J. Hale, late Editor of the American Ladies' Magazine, (which is now amalgamated with the Lady's Book,) will superintend the Literary Department of the Book. Mrs. Hale is too well known to the public to need eulogy from us. For nine years she has conducted the Magazine, which she originated. . . . It will therefore be perceived that a new era in the work has been commenced."

December 1836 was coming to an end, and publisher Louis Godey—owner of a Philadelphia publication, the *Lady's Book*—was addressing his readers about changes coming the following month to his publication, including his desire to fill future editions of his magazine with original material only. The energetic, plump, boastful publisher with a knack for marketing had worked in newspapers, where he had been trained as a "scissors editor"—clipping and reusing previously published material, often without attribution or payment to the original author and publication. He had run a newsstand-cum-bookshop before founding his magazine. Spread thin, he now desperately needed assistance and had approached Hale years earlier about working with him. Now he had finally managed to woo her to his publication—but not yet to Philadelphia.

As Hale's tenure as editor began in 1837, she initially decided to stay in Boston rather than move to Philadelphia, then the center of the publishing world and home to Godey's business—telecommuting without the "tele" part. Her son Horatio, a budding linguist, would soon graduate Harvard and set off on an international expedition for South America, New South Wales, and beyond. Her youngest, William, was to enter his brother's alma mater.

After the merger with Godey, Hale had not only a business partner but access to a much larger audience. It was as mutually beneficial a relationship as one could want. Godey had managed to decrease his workload and had hired a well-respected, highly connected, increasingly popular, and now *experienced* magazine editor, to boot. Hale, for her part, stood to amplify her already impressive voice.

She took no time exploiting this new position. In November of her first year at the helm of the *Lady's Book*, she penned an editorial on one of her favorite subjects.

"That merry anniversary, our Thanksgiving, has changed, to us, the gloomy aspect of the season, and made November (in which month the Thanksgiving should always be held) one of the brightest and best months in the year. . . ."

Hale also referred to December's festival (read "Christmas") as "peculiar" and bemoaned its eclipsing of her favorite annual holiday, one she considered linked to the "noble patrimony" of her Puritan Fathers. The Puritans did not embrace Christmas, considering it too closely linked to pagan rituals. They instead centered their annual seasonal celebration on the fall harvest. Many northern states, in addition to declared days of thanksgiving and prayer, had long celebrated an annual day of *general* thanksgiving, a date that roved around the end of the calendar, depending on the year and the location. By the middle of the nineteenth century, the practice had begun to spread west and south as well.

"The noble annual feast day of our Thanksgiving resembles, in some respects, the Feast of Pentecost, which was, in fact, the yearly season of Thanksgiving with the Jews. [Thanksgiving] might, without inconvenience, be observed on the same day of November, say the last Thursday in the month, throughout all New England; and also in our sister states, who have engrafted it upon *their* social system. It would then have a national character, which would, eventually, induce all the states to join in the commemoration of 'In-gathering,' which it celebrates. It is a festival which will never become obsolete, for it cherishes the best affections of the heart—the social and domestic ties. It calls together the dispersed members of the family circle, and brings plenty, joy and gladness to the dwellings of the poor and lowly. . . . The moral effect of this simple festival is essentially good."

And though Hale was not visibly or vocally aligned with the growing suffrage movement, she was not shy about extolling the rights and works of other women in her pages as well. In an editorial titled "Rights of Married Women," also published in her first year as editor of *Lady's Book*, she denounced laws dictating a woman's limited rights to property—even that which was rightfully and solely hers *prior* to marriage. As she had written years earlier in her annual reports to the Seaman's Aid Society, she abhorred the modern American practice that gave "to the husband uncontrolled power over the property of his wife. Though she possessed a million of dollars before she marries, she cannot, after she is a wife, dispose of a dollar in her own right . . ."

She continued in this vein in "Rights of Married Women": "The barbarous custom of wresting from woman whatever she possesses, whether by inheritance, donation or her own industry," Hale wrote, "and conferring it all upon the man she marries, to be used at his discretion and will, perhaps wasted on his wicked indulgences, without allowing her any control or redress, is such a monstrous perversion of *justice* by *law*."

Hale continued publishing her own books on the side, and promoting the work of other women. The year she moved to Godey's she published *The Ladies' Wreath*, a collection of writings of women poets, among them noted poet and essayist Lydia Huntley Sigourney, who also worked as an editor at *Lady's Book*. *The Ladies' Wreath* included notes for "young ladies" and was, as Hale declared on the title page, "A Gift-Book for All Seasons."

"I am aware that there are critics, who always speak of the 'true feminine style,' as though there was only one manner in which ladies could properly write poetry," she wrote in her preface, inviting readers to compare the styles of her chosen authors. "The delicate shades of genius are as varied and distinctly marked in the one sex as its bold outlines are in the other. There are more varieties of the rose than of the oak."

And within the pages of *Godey's* that year was a piece by author Harriet Beecher Stowe titled "Old Father Morris," which Stowe followed the next year with "Trials of a Housekeeper." Hale's ability to share women's writing was a cherished ideal.

"The wish to promote the reputation of my own sex and my own country, were among the earliest mental emotions I can recollect," Hale wrote in *The Ladies' Wreath*, "and had I then been told that it would be my good fortune to gather even this humble Wreath of poetical flowers from the productions of female writers, I should have thought it the height of felicity."

It was an active first year, in and outside the magazine. She spent Christmas with her children, save for her son Horatio, who was off exploring the Antarctic. She was already finding it hard to manage her Philadelphia workload while living in Boston. A move was clearly on the horizon, but it had to be delayed, not by obligation or preference but rather by grief. After fighting in the second Seminole War, Hale's son David and his artillery regiment were transferred to the northern reaches of the United States, in New York near Plattsburgh. There, the son on whom Hale had heavily relied as a single mother—emotionally and sometimes financially—became ill and died within days from what a superior officer described as an "unexpected and sudden effusion of the lungs."

"Lieutenant Hale was universally beloved by his brother

officers," the notice in the *Plattsburgh Republican* read, mourning the premature death of this "young, gallant, and enterprising" military man. His fellow officers erected a monument to him in Plattsburgh's Riverside Cemetery. The inscription read, in part: "He was amiable, brave, and talented."

A bereft Hale wrote to her Godey colleagues, who in turn shared her letter with readers.

"It is not a common loss that I mourn," Hale wrote.

> *My son was so noble and disinterested, that his character would not fail of exciting the affection of all who knew him, and to me his life has been one unbroken scene of obedience, love and generosity. I depended on him as a friend who would never disappoint me, and as the protector of my daughters and young son.—His death has destroyed all my plans of life; and though I know and feel that it is all right, that God, who gave me such a precious blessing, knew the best time to recall him, yet I cannot, at once, summon fortitude to enter on the occupations of a world so dark and desolate as it now appears.*

Though Hale eventually resumed her editorial duties, she further postponed her plans to move to Philadelphia. Then, in 1841, roughly four years into her tenure with Godey, with her son Horatio finally on his way home from his travels, Josepha in Georgia training to be a teacher, and William graduating from Harvard—second in his class, no less—the timing at last seemed right. Hale, challenged by managing the growing *Lady's Book* from afar, decided to move with her daughter Frances to Philadelphia.

Hale's time at *Godey's* would impact not just her life but those of countless others, male and female, across the country. She was, whether she had set out to be or not, establishing herself as both a literary and domestic tastemaker. She became an influencer, not only of fashion, manners, and the well-set table but also of tradition.

She proved to be remarkably prescient when it came to identifying cultural shifts. Two years after Queen Victoria ascended the throne of England at just eighteen years of age, Hale remarked, "Victoria's reign will be one of the longest in English annals. . . . She may so stamp her influence on the period in which she flourishes, that history shall speak of it as her own. It will be the Victorian, as a former one now is the Elizabethan age."

But the cultural institution that truly obsessed her was one that she knew she could better use her growing readership to achieve.

This campaign would not be limited to the pages of her magazine, though that platform afforded her unprecedented access to thousands upon thousands of eyes and minds. That wasn't going to be enough. She, herself, would write letters. To governors, to the heads of existing territories, and to presidents. She had what would seem a simple request. Would they consider uniting, as one nation, on the last Thursday of November each year to give thanks? For their country, for all they had, whether in times of scarcity or abundance?

To her, that day was an obvious choice—that was the very day that President George Washington had chosen.

CHAPTER 4

PRESIDENTS AND PROCLAMATIONS

I f George Washington was an inspiring leader on the battlefield, he was more reluctant to take charge once his weary boots were far from the action.

For some, including Congress, Washington would be the perfect choice to lead a country that couldn't quite agree on how to govern itself just yet. Washington was already serving as the president of the Constitutional Convention, a group of delegates tasked with hammering out a new constitution for the United States. And despite the bloodshed and anti-monarchical vitriol spewed during the Revolutionary War, it was ironic that some delegates—brash New Yorker Alexander Hamilton among them—favored a structure of government resembling that of England. Washington, for his part, was not overly keen to head up a new country after years spent in battle. There was a long road ahead.

If elected, the man who had no part in signing the Declaration of Independence, but who had so great a role in securing the independence it set forth, would now preside over a country held together by not only a brand-new constitution, but a highly contested one at that. The document made no mention of women. It counted enslaved people as equal to three-fifths of those who were white. Representation—a sticking point while under British rule and in many ways the scale-tipping impetus for the revolution itself—remained a key issue. Smaller states worried they would lose their voice alongside larger, more populous ones. The populous states didn't want those with fewer citizens dictating policy. Finally, on September 17, 1787, after cantankerous debates that nearly broke apart the freshly formed country, the Constitutional Convention voted to accept the Constitution of the United States of America. This document was signed by the thirty-nine of the original fifty-five convention delegates.

However, the battle was not over; the hard-fought document still had significant political hurdles to clear before it became the law of the land. Ratification challenges loomed up and down the coast, with states threatening to remain holdouts until amendments guaranteeing the rights of citizens were added to the document. Then, finally, on June 21, 1788, roughly four months before Sarah Josepha Buell's birth, her home state of New Hampshire became the ninth of the thirteen states to ratify the document, placing the framework of this new government fully into effect throughout the former colonies. The infighting among states and their representatives was not over, of course, and a bill of rights would soon be tacked on to address lingering issues.

Amending the Constitution in such a manner would continue to the present day, with each additional tweak often a sign of changing American values and expanding minds, ideally in keeping with an increasing and increasingly diverse nation.

The new constitution laid the groundwork for the first-ever quadrennial election, and Washington's election was a unanimous one. The day of his inauguration, April 30, 1789, was exceptionally celebratory. From the gunfire salutes at sunrise over his namesake military installation of Fort George, to the swearing in before hundreds of onlookers and foreign dignitaries at Federal Hall in New York City by his vice president, John Adams, to his delivery of the inaugural "inaugural" address in that same building's Senate chamber, the merrymaking continued. Church bells rang throughout the city and a new—if questionable—era in this new country began. At the time of Washington's inauguration, North Carolina and Rhode Island had yet to ratify the U.S. Constitution.

Political fracturing and factions showed the potential to grow into full party rifts. There were attacks along the borders, debtor prisons were chock-full of residents, and real estate bubbles burst that found even members of Congress upside down on their investments in this supposedly booming land.

And yet.

Within his very first year in office, and with internal struggling and external threats looming on the political horizon and waiting at porous frontier borders, the president of these tenuously united states made a proclamation of a decidedly unpolitical kind. It spoke not of treaties and policies or polemics but rather of gratitude and thanks. There would, he proclaimed, throughout each and every one of the thirteen states, be a national day of general thanksgiving.

Hale would have had no recollection of the first-ever thanksgiving proclamation issued by a president of the United States of America. She would have been on her family's farm outside Newport, New Hampshire, catching perhaps her first glimpses of late-afternoon autumn light dancing on the meandering currents of the Sugar River. Her parents and her brother were still alive, harvest was upon them, and young Sarah Josepha Buell would have been just one year old.

It was not the first time a proclamation of this sort had been issued in the colonies. The concept of unifying thanksgivings for all "Americans," such as they were during the revolution, predated the signing of the Constitution. During the war, proclamations of thanksgivings might follow significant successes in the struggle for independence and not necessarily those of successful harvests. For example, as Continental Congress member John Adams noted in his diary on July 24, 1766: "Thanksgiving for the Repeal of the Stamp-Act."

Years later, in the midst of war, the Continental Congress proclaimed a thanksgiving throughout the colonies. On October 21, 1777, just four days after British General John Burgoyne's surrender at Saratoga, New York, to General Horatio Gates—under whose command Hale's father, Gordon Buell, had served—noted Philadelphia surgeon Dr. Benjamin Rush penned a note to Adams:

"Adieu!" Rush wrote his friend and congressional colleague. "The good Christians and true Whigs expect a recommendation from Congress for a day of public thanksgiving for our Victories in the North. Let it be the same day for the whole continent."

John Adams's wife, Abigail, also contacted her husband upon hearing of the surrender, writing, "The joyfull News of the Surrender of General Burgoin and all his Army to our Victorious Troops prompted me to take a ride this afternoon with my daughter to Town to join to morrow with my Friends in thanksgiving and praise to the Supreem Being who hath so remarkably delivered our Enimies into our Hands."

Having a predominant hand in that particular proclamation was member of Congress and legendary ale namesake Samuel Adams, who, with some assistance from congressmen Richard Henry Lee of Virginia and Daniel Roberdeau from Pennsylvania, proclaimed Thursday, December 18, 1777, a "day of thanksgiving" as God had seen to "prosper the means used for the support of our troops and to crown our arms with most signal success." The proclamation intended that "with one heart and one voice the good people may express the grateful feelings of their hearts."

Roughly a year later, in 1778, statesman Samuel Adams's pen was also behind the congressional proclamation establishing December 30 of that year a day of thanksgiving for the support of the French for the American Revolution. These observances crossed cultural lines as well. Nearly three years later, in 1781, John Adams wrote Charles W. F. Dumas, a French-born agent for the Americans living in Holland, who had developed the first cipher used diplomatically by the Continental Congress. "The French Troops winter in Virginia," Adams wrote. "G. Washington returns to North River, to join the Body, which was left on the North River under General Heath. Our Countrymen will keep thanksgiving as devoutly as their Allies sing *Te Deum*." This, in reference to a Latin thanksgiving prayer long invoked by Catholics in France and elsewhere. Again, thanksgiving in this sense was essentially a penitent one, one of giving thanks in prayer.

The ratification of the Treaty of Paris came in January 1784, the official end of the Revolutionary War. And the first thanksgiving proclaimed by the fledgling American government as independent from British rule was set for November 26, 1784. The observance of public thanksgiving for the peace is one that extended across the pond as well. In July 1784, while in London, Abigail Adams wrote her friend Elizabeth Smith Shaw stating, "This is a day set apart for publick thanksgiving for the peace. The Shops are all shut and there is more the appearance of Solemnnity than on the Sabbeth."

Washington had his own thoughts on thanksgiving. The August following the start of his first term, Washington had written one of his trusted advisers, Virginia representative James Madison, about approaching the Senate with regard to proclaiming a national day of thanksgiving. Then in September, Elias Boudinot of New Jersey introduced a resolution in the House of Representatives "to request that [the president] would recommend to the people of the United States a day of public thanksgiving and prayer." President George Washington's proclamation, the first national proclamation ever issued by a president of the United States, arrived October 3, 1789, and read:

> Whereas it is the duty of all Nations to acknowledge the providence of Almighty God, to obey his will, to be grateful for his benefits, and humbly to implore his protection and favor—and whereas both Houses of Congress have by their joint Committee requested me "to recommend to the People of the United States a day of public thanksgiving and prayer to be observed by acknowledging with grateful hearts the many signal favors of Almighty God especially by affording them an opportunity peaceably to establish a form of government for their safety and happiness."
>
> Now therefore I do recommend and assign Thursday the 26th day of November next to be devoted by the People of these States to the service of that great and glorious Being, who is the beneficent Author of all the good that was, that is, or that will be—That we may then all unite in rendering unto him our sincere and humble thanks—for his kind care and protection of the People of this Country previous to their becoming a Nation—for the signal and manifold mercies, and the favorable interpositions of his

Providence which we experienced in the course and conclusion of the late war—for the great degree of tranquility, union, and plenty, which we have since enjoyed—for the peaceable and rational manner, in which we have been enabled to establish constitutions of government for our safety and happiness, and particularly the national One now lately instituted—for the civil and religious liberty with which we are blessed; and the means we have of acquiring and diffusing useful knowledge; and in general for all the great and various favors which he hath been pleased to confer upon us. . . .

Given under my hand at the City of New York the third day of October in the year of our Lord 1789.

In covering the proclamation, newspapers across the thirteen states reported it as a day of *reflection* and *service*—not feasting.

"Thursday 26th," Washington wrote in his diary in November 1789. "Being the day appointed for a thanksgiving I went to St. Paul's Chapel though it was most inclement and stormy—but few people at Church." Washington also spent seven pounds, four shillings, and ten pence to buy beer and other provisions for debtor prisoners at the New York City jail, then located next to the City Alms House on the street known as Broad Way.

The first thanksgiving under the new Constitution was

not entirely warmly received and its wording rubbed some the wrong way, as continued indications of conflict regarding the rights of states within this new union were proving to be an issue that showed little sign of abating. Thomas Tudor Tucker of South Carolina, for example, felt that those living in America "may not be inclined to return thanks for a Constitution until they have experienced that it promotes their safety and happiness. . . . If a day of thanksgiving must take place, let it be done by the authority of the several States; they know best what reason their constituents have to be pleased with the establishment of this Constitution." Representative Aedanus. Burke, also of South Carolina, himself recoiled at what he felt to be the "mimicking of European customs where they made a mere mockery of thanksgivings."

After Washington's proclamation in 1789, many state leaders continued to proclaim their own individual thanksgivings, as many of them already had become accustomed to, often choosing dates to suit their own calendars, harvest related or not. In 1794, in his role as governor of Massachusetts, Samuel Adams issued a proclamation in October for a "Day of Public Thanksgiving," calling on ministers of all faiths to gather with members of their congregations throughout the state. "And I do earnestly recommend that all such labor and recitations as are not consistent with the solemnity of the occasion may be carefully suspended on the said day."

In 1795, Washington issued another proclamation for a national day of thanksgiving throughout the country, but this time it was issued on New Year's Day and set a day for thanksgiving in February. Washington cited the many reasons the country had to be thankful: America was not at war. There was thanks to be given for what Washington referred to as a "great degree of internal tranquility," and he wanted to offer thanks for the "suppression of an insurrection which so wantonly threatened it." This was a reference to the Whiskey Rebellion of 1794, which saw farmers and distillers in Pennsylvania rising in protest of a federal tax on their product. "I George Washington President of the United States do recommend to all Religious Societies and Denominations and to all persons whomsoever, within the United States to set apart and observe Thursday, the nineteenth day of February next, as a day of public Thanksgiving and prayer."

Washington concluded with calls for humility and charity as well as gratitude. He poignantly noted that citizens should be preserved from "the arrogance of prosperity and from hazarding the advantages we enjoy by delusive pursuits." Individuals should seek to "merit the continuance of his favors, but not abusing them, by our gratitude for them, and by a correspondent conduct as citizens and as men." He mentioned that in doing so, America might "render this Country more and more as a safe and propitious asylum for the unfortunate of other Countries," and encouraged, again, charity, that through pious habits his compatriots could seek to "impart all the blessings we possess, or ask for ourselves, to the whole family of mankind."

Individual proclamations throughout the states continued. Then after ascending to the most powerful position in the country in 1797, President John Adams took an even more solemn tack in his proclamation, which he issued on March 23, 1798.

"I do hereby recommend, that *Wednesday, the Ninth Day of May* next be observed throughout the United States, as a day of Solemn Humiliation, Fasting and Prayer," Adams wrote. The Puritan tradition of spring fasting was an established one in New England, and John Adams was decidedly of Puritan stock, even if his religious views had evolved in a more Unitarian and Presbyterian direction. Adams hoped for the health of people and that agriculture, commerce, and arts be "blessed and prospered . . . and that the Blessings of Peace, Freedom, and Pure Religion, may be speedily extended to all the Nations of the Earth." He concluded: "Finally I recommend that on the said day, the Duties of Humiliation and Prayer be accompanied by fervent Thanksgiving." He followed suit the next April of 1799.

However, when Thomas Jefferson soundly beat John Adams to win the presidency in 1800, the Virginia planter, inventor, and violinist would issue no such proclamation. He was staunchly devoted to the separation of church and state. He shared those thoughts in writing with Reverend Samuel Miller, Presbyterian theologian and professor at the Princeton Theological Seminary, writing from Washington on January 23, 1808:

> *Sir, I have duly received your favor of the 18th*
> *and am thankful to you for having written it,*
> *because it is more agreeable to prevent than to*
> *refuse what I do not think myself authorized to*

comply with. I consider the government of the US as interdicted by the constitution from intermeddling with religious institutions, their doctrines, discipline, or exercises. This results not only from the provision that no law shall be made respecting the establishment, or free exercise, of religion, but from that also which reserves to the states the powers not delegated to the US. . . . Fasting & prayer are religious exercises. The enjoining them an act of discipline, every religious society has a right to determine for itself the times for these exercises & the objects proper for them, according to their own particular tenets; and this right can never be safer than in their own hands, where the constitution has deposited it.

Jefferson also acknowledged the actions of his predecessors—both of whom had issued their own proclamations—then continued: "Be this as it may, every one must act according to the dictates of his own reason, & mine tells me that civil powers alone have been given to the President of the US and no authority to direct the religious exercises of his constituents."

Four years later, in 1812, former president John Adams reflected on the tone of his own proclamation, again writing his friend Benjamin Rush:

The National Fast, reccommended by me turned me out of Office. It was connected with, the general

*Assembly of the Presbyterian Church, which I had
no concern in. That assembly has allarmed and
alienated Quakers, Anabaptists Mennonists,
Moravians, Sweedenborgians, Methodist,
Catholicks, Protestant Episcopalians, Arians
Socinians, Arminians & &c. Atheists and Deists
might be added. A general Suspicion prevailed that
the Presbyterian Church was ambitious and aimed
at an Establishment as a National Church. I was
represented as a Presbyterian and at the head of
this political and ecclesiastical Project. The Secret
Whisper ran through them all the Sects "Let Us
have Jefferson, Madison, Burr, any body, whether
they be Philosophers, Deist or even Atheists, rather
than a Presbyterian President." This Principle is at
the Bottom of the Unpopularity of national Fasts
and Thanksgivings, Nothing is more dreaded than
the National Government meddling with Religion.
This wild Letter I very much fear, contains Seeds of
an Ecclesiastical History of the U.S. for a Century
to come.*

Later, Adams's grandson—and future biographer—
Charles Francis Adams, Sr., described thanksgiving in his
diary on November 26, 1828, as "the substitute of the Puritans for Christmas." On Christmas of that year, during the
presidential term of his father, John Quincy Adams, the
twenty-one-year-old Charles lamented that while he had
looked to Christmas as a time for pleasure and happiness,

"These ideas are not congenial here, for with the customs of the Puritans they transfer to Thanksgiving, an Institution of their own, what ought to come at Christmas and New Year."

For many communities the day *after* the state-declared annual thanksgiving was traditionally much more revelatory. A day of thanksgiving would be declared and solemnly observed, with labor and recreation frowned upon. The day after featured, as one Connecticut newspaper described it, "widely different amusements to suit all kinds of folks. In shooting turkeys and hens, visiting the neighbors, and taking a nearer view of the eclipsed luxuries of the day before."

If Charles Francis Adams bewailed thanksgiving's usurping of Christmas cheer, he nevertheless believed in gratitude as an action worth effort, writing on Thursday, November 29, 1832, of the "practice of thankfulness."

"Suffering in this world is natural. Prosperity is not so, if long continued. Therefore man must not complain if he experiences what he was born to experience, and he must be thankful for the good gifts which he has no right to claim."

Two years later, when Massachusetts celebrated thanksgiving on November 27, 1834, he complained in his diary: "New England never has been able to throw off the sad colored livery which distinguished its origin," adding that he declined to go to a friend's home where he would have to partake of "the excessive table which is the only amusement of a Thanksgiving day in most families."

As for New Englander Hale, she had developed a passion for both—thankfulness *and* an excessive table. But gubernatorial proclamations were not enough, in her opinion. She would continue to make her case in the *Lady's Book* for an annual holiday. She knew it was time to take it beyond the pages of the magazine and to the only office in the country that could truly make this day of thanks all that she hoped it could be. Every year. Always.

CHAPTER 5

NOW MORE THAN EVER

B ut now to my dinner . . ."
Or so began Hale's extravagant description of the
kind of celebration she hoped would soon be a national pastime. She knew exactly how to lay out an "excessive table." Hale had, in fact, described in spectacular detail
that very species of table seven years earlier in her novel
Northwood; or, A Tale of New England, in which the better
part of an entire chapter is devoted to a thanksgiving dinner.

First, she delves into decadent detail about the table in
the parlor: "A long table, formed by placing two of the ordinary size together . . . covered with a damask cloth." She
extols the whiteness and texture of the cloth, noting that
everyone in the family would get to enjoy the fine linen:
"every child having a seat on this occasion; and the more the
better, it being considered an honor for a man to sit down to
his Thanksgiving supper surrounded by a large family."

Despite the fact that earlier in the chapter Hale claims that "the description of a feast is a kind of literary treat, which I never much relished," she makes an exception "as this was a Thanksgiving entertainment, one which was never before, I believe, served up in style to *novel* epicures, I may venture to mention some of the peculiarities of the festival."

She then launches into descriptions of the food that were beyond indulgent:

"The roasted turkey took precedence on this occasion, being placed at the head of the table; and well did it become its lordly station, sending forth the rich odor of its savory stuffing, and finely covered with the frost of the basting. At the foot of the board a sirloin of beef, flanked on either side by a leg of pork and loin of mutton, seemed placed as a bastion to defend innumerable bowls of gravy and plates of vegetables disposed in that quarter. A goose and pair of ducklings occupied side stations on the table; the middle being graced, as it always is on such occasions, by that rich burgomaster of the provisions, called a chicken pie." She describes that pie as "wholly formed of the choicest parts of the fowls, enriched and seasoned with a profusion of butter and pepper, and covered with an excellent puff paste, is, like the celebrated pumpkin pie, an indispensable part of a good and true Yankee Thanksgiving."

Hale did not stop there. There were "plates of pickles, preserves, and butter," as well as seasonings, wine, a "huge plum pudding, custards and pies of every name and description ever known in Yankee land. . . . [S]everal kinds of rich cake, and a variety of sweetmeats and fruits." Currant wine.

Ginger beer. Tumblers and sideboards and conversation and thanks.

The four food pillars of Thanksgiving—turkey, cranberries, stuffing, and pumpkin pie—already had a foothold in American cuisine. Native Americans had long eaten cranberries, fresh and dried. In addition to their vitamin C, they contain benzoic acid, a natural preservative, making them ideal for storage. Stuffing, or "forcemeat" (from the French *farce*), was an established culinary practice in England and continental Europe that had made its way to the tables of settlers on this continent. Eating fowl had a long tradition in many parts of the world, from the finest of tables—sixty-six were served up to Catherine de Medici in 1549—to the simplest of settlements, eaten wild or domesticated. And pie from pumpkin also had a history in England. In North America the gourds grow well and are harvested in late summer or early fall—making them ripe for the holiday. A recipe for the treat can be found in America's earliest known cookbook, *American Cookery*, published by Amelia Simmons in 1796.

But until Hale put pen to paper in 1827, no American writer had ever deigned to describe in such deliciously effusive detail the components of a Yankee thanksgiving.

Her characters sat around a table to delight in the kind of over-the-top and magnificent feast that would eventually grace tables across the United States each November. However, despite the various proclamations to date, both state and national, there was still no nationally established thanksgiving holiday in November. And Hale's book was utter fiction.

Whether she realized it or not, Hale was positioning herself as a domestic arts goddess, an arbiter of not just manners but, she hoped, traditions that transcended differences. The foods eaten, the setting, and the decor of the table were critical, as was the idea of giving thanks together, as a nation. She wanted to take what had been an ad hoc, regionally malleable event and transform it into a national holiday.

She would need to petition those in a position to help her. People in power. Elected officials. In the meantime, the "editress," as she often called herself, would continue to preach to her readership in the pages of *Godey's Lady's Book*. The magazine made a fine pulpit, its circulation increasing by the thousands each year under Hale's editorship. Magazines were precious commodities and often shared by and among friends. Considering that a subscriber might share their "book" with five neighbors, Hale could easily have been preaching her thanksgiving gospel to an audience of hundreds of thousands of readers, in a time when the country's population totaled just over seventeen million.

Her personal life in the early days after moving to Philadelphia—even in the wake of her son David's death—was fruitful. Her family had suffered a loss but was growing as well. Her daughter Frances Ann married Philadelphia physician and naval surgeon Dr. Lewis Boudinot Hunter, grandson of Declaration of Independence signer Richard Stockton. This aspect of her son-in-law's lineage must have surely pleased Hale, to whom the Union meant so much. "Mary's Lamb" appeared in print yet again, this time in *My Little Song Book*, and its popularity continued to grow. The seeds of a former crusade—her desire to see the completion of the Bunker Hill Monument—came to fruition. Though her initial outreach to readers raised only $3,000, Hale had not been deterred. She had organized a fair at Quincy Hall that lasted seven days, where women sold crafts, jams, baked goods, and more. Hale created a special publication for the fair—aptly titled "The Monument"—full of short poems and anecdotes, which raised more than $500 on its own. By the end of the fair, not only had Hale's venture raised $30,000 in sales, but its success inspired other deep-pocketed donors, bringing the total raised to well over $50,000. Those who had initially scoffed at the idea that women could raise the required sum where men had failed were suitably chastened. Hale attended the monument's dedication—thirteen years after she first began raising awareness and money for it.

The middle of the century brought a profusion of activism around the area of women's rights. The Woman's Rights Convention—the first of its kind—was held in 1848 in Seneca Falls, New York. This was driven by the efforts of Elizabeth Cady Stanton, Quaker preacher Lucretia Coffin Mott, Mary M'Clintock (who along with Mott organized the Philadelphia Female Anti-Slavery Society), Martha Coffin Wright (who also ran a station on the Underground Railroad), and Quaker activist Jane Hunt. The overlap between the abolitionist movement and the women's rights movement was significant, with abolitionist, statesman, and author Frederick Douglass speaking at Seneca Falls as well. Hale did not attend or cover the event.

"We have said little of the 'Rights of Woman,'" Hale wrote sometime after the convention. "Her first right is to education in its widest sense—to such education as will give her the full development of all her personal, mental, and moral qualities. Having that, there will be no longer any questions about her rights; and rights are liable to be perverted to wrongs when we are incapable of rightly exercising them. . . . The *Lady's Book* . . . was the first avowed advocate of the holy cause of women's intellectual progress; it has been the pioneer in the wonderful change of public sentiment respecting female education, and the employment of female talent in educating the young. We intend to go on, sustained and accelerated by this universal encouragement, till our grand aim is accomplished, till *female education* shall receive the same careful attention and liberal support from public legislation as are bestowed on that of the other sex."

As tirelessly as Hale may have advocated, in action and voice, for women's education and marital rights, she stopped far short of being a suffragette. Hale would never lobby for the blanket rights of women. Not long after the Seneca convention, she wrote a column titled "How American Women Should Vote." In it, Hale describes a woman—unnamed, and quite possibly fictional—with a husband and six sons. The woman explains, "I control seven votes; why should I desire to cast one myself?" Hale concludes, "This is the way American women should vote, namely, by influencing rightly the votes of men."

In the pages of her magazine, she not only supported education for women but also pressed for the advancement of women in fields where they were still unwelcome, such as medicine. She mocked reports of male students complaining about feeling uncomfortable studying alongside women, and that women could not always be relied upon to be available due to their responsibilities at home. Hale heralded Elizabeth Blackwell, the first woman to receive a medical degree in the United States, when she graduated in 1849.

Hale in theory and in practice might seem rather contrarian. In appearance, she was ever the Victorian: her side curls, bustles, crinoline, and pantalets. And yet in her pages, alongside elaborate instructions for broiling meat or using dress patterns, she would protest inequities against women in the fields of education and property rights. She was, in her way, almost subtle—and perhaps more subversive. She used her fictional writings and her ladies' publication to rally for change, and supported other women as a growing force in the media.

Heading into 1850, a year that would see *Godey's* circulation hit sixty thousand subscribers, Louis Godey knew on whose shoulders his magazine's success rested. "This department is under the control of Mrs. Sarah Josepha Hale," he wrote, "whose name alone is a sufficient guarantee for the propriety of the Lady's Book." Never short on bombast, however, Godey had on a separate occasion declared the magazine and its growing circulation as the "most extraordinary instance of success that has ever been recorded!" and "Nearly double that of any other magazine." True or not, it was a good time to publish a periodical. Following the Panic of 1837, which saw the downfall of many book publishing outfits, magazines came into their own. *Godey's, Graham's,*

Peterson's . . . magazines, especially those for women, were becoming a force in American culture.

This was the beginning of the era of the professional writer, ones who were paid for their work and supported themselves largely on their earnings, and Hale continued her relationship with both burgeoning and established writers. In one five-year stretch in the 1840s, she published "Drowne's Wooden Image," by Nathaniel Hawthorne; three poems by Ralph Waldo Emerson; and works by Oliver Wendell Holmes Sr., Harriet Beecher Stowe, William Cullen Bryant, Washington Irving, James Russell Lowell, John Greenleaf Whittier, and John Quincy Adams. Hale's son Horatio was acquainted with Henry Wadsworth Longfellow, and Hale included his poem "The Twilight" in *The Opal: A Pure Gift for the Holy Days*, a Christmas annual she owned and edited. Later, she included more of Longfellow's poems in the magazine as well.

Hale also remained close with and regularly published Edgar Allan Poe. Poe would occasionally fire off a missive to the mother of his former classmate David Hale, at times taking inflammatory aim at other writers. For a time Poe had the brilliant idea of writing a monthly column for the *Lady's Book* titled "The Literati of New York City: Some Honest Opinions at Random Respecting Their Authorial Merits, with Occasional Words of Personality," under the byline Edgar A. Poe. His gossipy barbs soon elicited complaints from readers, publishers, and the maligned authors themselves, and Louis Godey—who wanted to sell magazines, not ruffle feathers—felt compelled to tell subscribers that Mr. Poe's views were entirely his own. Godey's column on the matter was, in essence, a nineteenth-century version of the still-oft-cited disclaimer: "The views and opinions presented are solely those of the author."

Despite such controversy, nothing could dislodge Poe's fictional work from Hale's publication. Over the years Hale would review his works and publish many of Poe's short stories and poems. Her January 1840 review of his two-volume work *Tales of the Grotesque and Arabesque* was published in such short order that she must have had access to something akin to an advance proof. The review in *Lady's Book*—valuable for any writer—said, "Mr. Poe is a writer of rare and various abilities. . . . The volumes now published, contain favorable specimens of Mr. Poe's powers, and cannot fail to impress all who read them, with a conviction of his genius." Possibly the most famous of his works to appear in the pages of *Lady's Book* was the first-ever printing of "The Cask of Amontillado." One can only imagine how the magazine's feminine readership took to the story of a vengeful nobleman who entombed his still-breathing rival in the subterranean alcove of a crypt. The last of his stories to appear in the *Lady's Book* was "Mellonta Tauta," issued in 1849, the year Poe died.

Godey and Hale were quite well suited, and Godey eventually began advertising some of her books for sale in his column, "Godey's Arm Chair." Subscribers could, if they so chose, buy mail-order copies of books, including *Mrs. Hale's*

Cook-Book and *Mrs. Hale's Household Receipt-Book*, which Godey described as "absolutely necessary for every housekeeper." If one wanted instruction on carving meat and fowl and "arranging the table for parties," then *Mrs. Hale's New Cook Book* was a better option. Of course *Mrs. Hale's Receipts for the Million* offered "useful, ornamental, and domestic arts." Price for each: one dollar. "Remember," Godey wrote his readers, "the Lady's book is not a mere luxury; it is a necessity." He offered her literary works for sale as well, with prices ranging from seventy-five cents to five dollars.

Over the years it hadn't all been perfect between the partners, but disagreements tended to resolve themselves. Hale fought against, for example, the inclusion of the increasingly popular tinted fashion plates in their publication. (This, perhaps, was little surprise given Hale's own all-black attire.) These hand-colored etchings and lithographs depicted the latest styles of dress. "Dress and personal appearance," Hale wrote her readers, "these, in a Lady's Book, as well as in real life, are important things. Character is displayed, yes! [M]oral taste and goodness, or their perversion, are indicated in dress." Finally she capitulated, and *Godey's* became one of the first and best publications to share these often French-inspired depictions of couture. (However, the publication advised against blindly chasing Parisian fashion trends.) More fashion-forward columns included those penned by one "Florence Fashionhunter."

As for hygiene, the magazine said a bath once a week was advisable, perhaps on Saturday, and it was arguably the first to advocate exercise for women, extolling the virtues of maintaining a healthy woman's figure—tight corsets to be eschewed. Hale's own ablutions were at once quite simple and strangely particular. Before going to bed, she soaked brown butcher's paper in apple vinegar and laid the wet strips near the corners of her eyes to ward off crow's-feet. She also made her own moisturizer from coconut milk, lard, and rose water.

The magazine's topics continued to run the gamut and notch notable publishing firsts. It featured stories on the skull-reading "science" of phrenology. It presented the audacious concept of wearing white on one's wedding day—as Queen Victoria had when marrying Prince Albert. It also included some of the earliest, and certainly most widely visible, illustrations of a Christmas tree in any American publication. Hale was also was credited with coining the phrase "domestic science."

And as Hale's influence grew over the years, she had yet to realize what she referred to as "one of the strongest wishes of my heart."

Beyond *Northwood*, Hale had written about the idea of a national thanksgiving either directly as editor or indirectly via the dialogue of fictional characters that appeared in the pages of the magazine. She offered her magazine subscribers countless hostess suggestions and "receipts" (recipes), with dishes ranging from *soodjee*, a fish dish, to cider-soaked ham and "Lafayette Ducks with Snow-Balls" (a sweet-starchy mix of boiled rice, raisins, sugar, and coffee).

Her fellow editor and New Englander, Massachusetts-raised Lydia Maria Child, shared Hale's love of the holiday and had published her own ode to the day, titled "The New-England Boy's Song About Thanksgiving Day." The poem first appeared in *Flowers for Children, II*. Though her prior publications attracted attention for their abolitionist stances, *Flowers* took a rather less controversial approach, and this poem's popularity would carry over decades and across the country, and the original verses would speak to Hale's heart:

Over the river, and through the wood,
To grandfather's house we go;
The horse knows the way,
To carry the sleigh,
Through the white and drifted snow.

Over the river, and through the wood,
To grandfather's house away!
We would not stop
For doll or top,
For 't is Thanksgiving day.

Over the river, and throgh the wood,
Oh, how the wind does blow!
It stings the toes,
And bites the nose,
As over the ground we go.

Over the river, and through the wood,
With a clear blue winter sky,

The dogs do bark,
And children hark,
As we go jingling by.

Over the river, and through the wood,
To have a first-rate play—
Hear the bells ring
Ting a ling ding,
Hurra for Thanksgiving day!

Over the river, and through the wood—
No matter for winds that blow;
Or if we get
The sleigh upset,
Into a bank of snow.

Over the river, and through the wood,
To see little John and Ann;
We will kiss them all,
And play snow-ball,
And stay as long as we can.

Over the river, and through
  the wood,
Trot fast, my dapple grey!
Spring over the ground,
Like a hunting hound!
For 't is Thanksgiving day!

Over the river, and through
  the wood,
And straight through the
  barn-yard gate;
We seem to go
Extremely slow,
It is so hard to wait.

Over the river, and through
  the wood—
Old Jowler hears our bells;

He shakes his pow,
With a loud bow wow,
And thus the news he tells.

Over the river, and through
  the wood—
When grandmother sees us
  come,
She will say, Oh dear,
The children are here,
Bring a pie for every one.

Over the river, and through
  the wood—
Now grandmother's cap I spy!
Hurra for the fun!
Is the pudding done?
Hurra for the pumpkin pie!

Hale began her letter-writing campaign to convince U.S. presidents of the merits of her cause with Virginian Zachary Taylor.

The twelfth president—"Old Rough and Ready," as the general of both the War of 1812 and the Mexican-American War was known—had taken office in 1849 after his predecessor, James K. Polk, had added substantially to the territories of the United States. Polk had done this in part by waging war with Mexico, and those territories gained—including what is now California, New Mexico, and Utah—were at the center of a growing and increasingly incendiary debate over whether slavery should be allowed to spread to the newly acquired lands.

Taylor, though a slaveholder himself, did not think slavery should be allowed in the new territories. As a military man, he may have been more likely to put down whispers of secession efforts with force rather than diplomacy. Taylor desired the growing Union to remain intact, making him the kind of president Hale must have thought would understand her desire for a unifying holiday. He did not. Taylor's term would be a short-lived one—a mere sixteen months. On July 9, 1850, he fell ill after taking a long walk on July 4 and eating a big bowl of cherries on a hot day. He died from cholera morbus, shocking the country, and Taylor's vice president, Millard Fillmore, ascended to the presidency.

Hale's efforts fared no better with Fillmore. Fillmore's term in office saw him strongly support the Compromise of 1850, but he also aligned himself with the proslavery camp in the enforcement of the Fugitive Slave Act. He soon joined up with the Know-Nothing Party, or American Party, an anti-immigrant, anti-Catholic party that promoted "native-born" rule. The Know Nothings ran Fillmore as their nominee for his reelection bid in 1856. He was unsuccessful. If the Compromise of 1850 staved off war for the time being, the existence of parties like the Know Nothings stood as evidence of increased nationalism and tensions over slavery, bellwethers that the Union Hale so loved was fracturing even further. The debate impacted her own publication as well. In 1850, Louis Godey fired writer and editor Grace Greenwood—also known as Sarah Jane Clarke—from her editorial position at the magazine after she published work in the abolitionist newspaper the *National Era*.

In 1852, during Fillmore's largely forgettable term, Hale reissued *Northwood* with a new title—*Northwood; or, Life North and South: Showing the True Character of Each*. Her favorite holiday remained on fine display in the new edition, and she took advantage of the reissue to amplify her campaign—via her characters, of course.

"Is Thanksgiving Day universally observed in America?" asks a visiting Englishman. "Not yet," his host replies, "but I trust it will become so. We have too few holidays. Thanksgiving like the Fourth of July should be considered a national festival and observed by all our people. . . . When it shall be observed, on the same day, throughout all the states and territories, it will be a grand spectacle of moral power and human happiness, such as the world has never witnessed."

Hale also added a new preface to *Northwood*, in which she referred to the novel as "an era in my life." She noted her own reliance on fiction to share some of her personal views. "*Northwood* was written when what is now known as 'Abolitionism' first began seriously to disturb the harmony between the South and the North," she wrote. She praised the importance of the Constitution and, above all else, that the Union remain intact. "The great error of those who would sever the Union rather than see a slave within its borders, is, that they forget the *master* is their brother, as well as the *servant*; and that the spirit which seeks to do good to all and evil to none is the only true Christian philanthropy." As before, her characters shared disparate views on the institution, from abhorrence to tolerance. "Slavery is, no doubt, a great evil," one of her characters writes in a journal, "so is despotic power; yet anarchy is worse than despotism; and to kill prisoners of war, or allow the poor to perish of hunger, is worse than servitude."

Hale seemed to hope that the slavery issue could be resolved without dividing the country in war. "Fiction derives its chief worth from the truths it teaches," she wrote in the preface. "I have aimed to set forth some important truths— their worth I leave to be estimated by the Reader."

Hale's reissuing of *Northwood* would eventually be seen as a response to another book published that year: *Uncle Tom's Cabin*. Harriet Beecher Stowe's bestselling book captivated the nation and brought the horrors of slavery in America into countless parlors and sitting rooms. *Uncle Tom's Cabin*—which would go on to be the bestselling novel of the nineteenth century—was quite different in tone from *Northwood* but had something in common with Hale's revised edition: Both discussed colonization.

"Never will the negro stand among men as a man, till he has earned for himself that title in his own country— magnificent Africa—which God has given him as a rich inheritance," *Northwood* states. Some supporters of the controversial idea of colonization—considered at the time to be a more moderate stance than abolition—believed that emancipated slaves and freeborn persons of color would fare better if voluntarily relocated to a place where they could live as free citizens. One such location was Liberia, a settlement of the American Colonization Society (ACS). Founded in 1816, the ACS promoted raising funds in order to support this emigration to Africa. Toward the end of Hale's revised *Northwood*, one of her characters announces he intends "to help colonize Liberia. What a glorious prospect is there opened before the freed slave from America! . . . And if there is a country on earth where some future hero, greater even than our Washington, may arise, it is Africa."

Colonization had advocates and detractors from many different corners of the political landscape, from Quakers to slaveholders; and early supporters of the movement included former presidents and slaveholders Thomas Jefferson, James Madison, and James Monroe.

The same year that *Uncle Tom's Cabin* and the revised *Northwood* were published, Frederick Douglass shared his objections to this philosophy in a piece titled "The Colonization Scheme" in *Frederick Douglass' Paper*, stating, "There is no sentiment more universally entertained, nor more firmly held by the free colored people of the United States, than that this is their 'own, their native land,' and that here, (for good or for evil) their destiny is to be wrought out."

The following year, in 1853, Hale would publish *Liberia; or, Mr. Peyton's Experiments*, a fictional, book-length exploration of colonization. For those who opposed slavery but still could not envision a world in which white and Black people lived alongside one another peacefully and prosperously, separation seemed a solution, though a contentious one. Despite their prior editor-writer relationship, Hale did not write a review or notice for Stowe's *Uncle Tom's Cabin*—or any other antislavery works—in *Lady's Book*, though the magazine did review other anti-abolition books.

A year after *Liberia*'s publication, a man seeking to revive his political career would directly address this conflict during a speech delivered in Peoria, Illinois, stating: "If the negro is a *man*, why then my ancient faith teaches me that 'all men are created equal'; and that there can be no moral right in connection with one man's making a slave of another." In the same speech, he also said, "If all earthly power were given to me, I should not know what to do as to the existing institution. My first impulse would be to free all the slaves, and send them to Liberia,—to their own native land."

This soon-to-be presidential candidate would grapple with slavery for the rest of his life, and the emancipation of enslaved people would become his political legacy.

The success of my literary life has enabled me to educate my children liberally, as their father would have done," Hale wrote in the preface to the revised edition of *Northwood*, "and I hope the influence of the various productions I have sent forth has been in some degree beneficial to my own sex, and to the cause of sound literature and of pure morality."

To that end, a year later Hale published a collection of women's writings titled *Woman's Record; or, Sketches of All Distinguished Women, from "The Beginning" till A.D. 1850.* "The ninth wave of the nineteenth century," she wrote in the introduction, "is the Destiny of Woman."

Not to shirk her other editorial responsibilities, the same year *Northwood* was reissued Hale went so far as to introduce an exotic new word to her readers: "The word '*lingerie*,' which heads our article, will doubtless be unfamiliar to many of our readers, even though conversant with the

French language." The magazine was less than enthusiastic about another new trend: bloomers. Amelia Bloomer's blousy pantaloons, or "freedom dresses," were becoming all the rage—both inciting debate and garnering negative attention from those who held fast to the idea of a corseted lady. Choosing to keep initially mum on the topic, the magazine eventually had no choice but to acknowledge the enduring trend. Reversing course years after bloomers burst on the scene, the *Lady's Book* would feature what it called the "Metropolitan Gymnastic Costume," designed for exercise and outdoor activity.

As her readership indulged in the delights and subtleties of lacy undergarments, Hale remained steadfast in her thanksgiving quest. Decades had passed since she had penned her ode to the day in the pages of *Northwood*, and though no president so far had acquiesced to her plea, Hale continued imploring them, along with ambassadors, governors, and readers, to join her in establishing the national holiday. She always lobbied for the same day that George Washington had chosen back in 1789—the last Thursday of November.

She often shared notes of support that she had received from enthusiastic thanksgiving bandwagon jumpers in the magazine. Notes from dignitaries and ordinary citizens often described how they had observed the holiday at her suggestion. "Last year, twenty-nine States and all the Territories united in the festival," she wrote in 1852. "This year, we trust that Virginia and Vermont will come into this arrangement, and the Governors of each and all the States will appoint *Thursday, the 25th of November, as the Day of Thanksgiving.*"

Later in the issue she heralded the possibility of "Nearly twenty-five millions of people sitting down, as it were, together to a feast of joy and thankfulness."

In the 1852 election, Franklin Pierce emerged as victor, and perhaps Hale would have better luck with the fourteenth president of the United States, who happened to be a fellow New Hampshire native. She was proud that the Granite State was standing by the Union. "One cheering proof of the world's progress is the earnestness of those who are now working in the cause of humanity," Hale had written in the preface to the revised *Northwood*. Considered by many to be ineffectual, President Pierce backed the Kansas-Nebraska Act, which allowed residents of those territories to decide whether to allow slavery within their geographic boundaries. The fate of the Union seemed even more dismal.

However, as the fraying fabric holding the Union together began to tear, Hale was silent in her own magazine. This may not have been a choice. Louis Godey had a stated aversion to including politics in his publication. So any of Hale's thoughts and opinions of even the slightest political bent were left to the pages of her novels—which may have been where she preferred they reside. If there was a topic she was outspoken about, it was her desire for the Union to remain intact.

In an earlier series in the magazine, "Heroic Women of the Revolution," Hale managed to have some of her interviewees—whether they realized it or not—express her own stance in favor of keeping the nation together. When "A

Carolina Woman of the Revolution" was interviewed in *Lady's Book* in 1856, it included emphasis on that subject's roots in the North. She said that during the American Revolution, "An attack on the liberties of Massachusetts was viewed as an attack upon Carolina."

Unable to project leadership in trying times, Pierce became yet another one-term president. He was gone by 1857, along with Hale's hopes of a presidential thanksgiving proclamation.

In 1857, James Buchanan entered a difficult presidency as the slavery debate consumed America. He himself despised abolitionists. Though from the North, he often took a southern view of things, siding with his political allies. During Buchanan's presidency, Hale's editorials took a stronger stance. In 1859, one year before South Carolina's secession, she wrote an editorial titled "Our Thanksgiving Union":

"Seventy years ago the political union of the United States was consummated; in 1789, the thirteen original States, then forming the American Confederacy, became by the ratification of the Constitution, . . . the United American Nation. The flag of our country now numbers thirty-two stars. . . . God save the United States!" She then implored, "If every State should join in a union thanks-giving on the 24th of this month, would it not be a renewed pledge of love and loyalty to the Constitution of the United States, which guarantees peace, prosperity, progress, and perpetuity to our great Republic?"

If citizens were looking to James Buchanan to be the president who could pull the country together, "Old Buck" did not come through.

"Thanksgiving, like the Fourth of July, should be considered a national festival and observed by all our people," Hale wrote in the *Lady's Book* during Buchanan's term. "Let the last THURSDAY IN NOVEMBER be agreed upon as the DAY of American Thanksgiving in all the States of our Union, and the world would have a new epoch of hope, a new pledge of peace, and a new and brighter ray from the torch of Liberty than our Independence can furnish them, because our Union Thanksgiving would signify the moral unity of the American people."

Strong national leadership eluded the bachelor president. He had been reluctant to take the highest post in the land, writing before his campaign: "I had hoped for the nomination in 1844, again in 1848, and even in 1852, but now I would hesitate to take it. Before many years the abolitionists will bring war upon this land. It may come during the next presidential term."

II

TEARING APART
AND
COMING TOGETHER

GRATITUDE to benefactors is a well recognized virtue, to express it in some form or other, however imperfectly, is a duty to ourselves as well as to those who have helped us.

—FREDERICK DOUGLASS

CHAPTER 6

TO THESE BOUNTIES

A white flag flew over the small open boat as it crossed the waters. Rowed by enslaved men, the vessel was headed to Fort Sumter, which sat and sits still in Charleston's harbor. This was not the boat Major Robert Anderson was hoping for. That ship, the *Star of the West*, carrying much-needed food and other supplies, already had been detained in this, the January of 1861, by rebel forces, taking fire from both Fort Moultrie on Sullivan's Island and the Citadel Battery. Brigadier General P. G. T. Beauregard demanded Major Anderson surrender the fort to his Confederate forces. Anderson refused. Then, on April 12, 1861, Confederate forces fired from Fort Johnson on the northeast point of James Island in Charleston Harbor. The shots struck the walls of Fort Sumter, occupied by a garrison of United States forces led by Major Anderson.

The battle was a brief, violent, one-sided one. Anderson surrendered the fort the next day, on April 13. The first soldier to lose his life in the Civil War was not actually caught in the line of fire. He was an artilleryman, and a premature cannon discharge took his life. His death was an accident. In perhaps a growing reflection of the evolving character of the nation, the artilleryman was Private Daniel Hough, a recently immigrated Irishman.

James Buchanan did not ultimately turn out to be the kind of president who would lead the country away from internal conflict. His support of the Supreme Court's Dred Scott Decision—which declared that Black people were not citizens, that enslaved people were property, and that Congress could not prohibit slavery in the territories—as well as the decision itself, enraged abolitionists and widened the gulf between North and South. However, Buchanan had been absolutely correct in predicting the challenges his successor would have to face. That man was an Illinois lawyer named Abraham Lincoln.

In his quest for the Republican party nomination, Abraham Lincoln had bested powerful former Whig—and former New York governor—William H. Seward, a U.S. senator. The Whig Party had emerged in the wake of, and in opposition to, President Andrew Jackson and the tyranny they believed he represented. The 1860 election saw four candidates in the increasingly fractured United States: Lincoln, John C. Breckinridge of the Southern Democratic Party, John Bell of the Constitutional Union, and Stephen A. Douglas of the Northern Democratic Party. With their victory in the presidential election, Lincoln and his vice presidential running mate, Hannibal Hamlin, represented the first winning Republican ticket in decades dominated by Whigs. Lincoln had made it clear prior to the election that he opposed the further spread of slavery in the states, even if his own views on what to do once slavery was eradicated were continuing to evolve. Before the election, voters knew where he stood politically. And just a little over a month after Abraham Lincoln's November 6, 1860, victory, South Carolina became the first state to secede from the United States of America.

The newly elected president appointed his former party foe William H. Seward as his secretary of state. But by the time Lincoln was inaugurated on March 4, 1861, a total of seven states had already seceded to form the Confederate States of America, and appointed Jefferson Davis, Mexican-American War veteran and plantation owner, as their president. In April, Confederates attacked Fort Sumter and open war was upon the United States. Four more states would join the Confederate States of America before summer was over, bringing the total number of seceded states to eleven.

Sarah Josepha Hale saw the Union she cherished, the one her father had fought for and been injured during the Revolutionary War, come apart. Achieving a different result for her campaign now—a positive one—in the midst of all that was facing the still young and increasingly fragile nation and the president struggling to lead it seemed futile.

Yet Hale was not to be deterred. Somehow the conflict made taking time to pause and come together to give thanks as a nation all the more necessary. The president was besieged politically. Loyalties were splintering, rending communities to shreds, leaving them bristling with more animosity and tension than even during the time of the American Revolution. Now, anger was shattering the bonds of family and friendship, and the nation—not yet a century into its existence—seemed destined for a bloody dismantling.

Hale's use of press as pulpit had been a convenient, if not always effective, choice for her in her role as the editor of *Godey's Lady's Book*. Her success at rallying readers to various causes over the years must have been cheering to some degree. The growing cadre of governors and other leaders who supported her thanksgiving cause was surely satisfying. However, there could be no national holiday without the support of the commander in chief, and this particular commander in chief had a lot on his plate.

Similar to Hale, Lincoln had been, to a great extent, primarily self-educated. An avid reader, he was fond of the words of Edgar Allan Poe and poet-polymath Oliver Wendell Holmes, both of whom Hale had published in her magazines and, over the years, befriended as well. Where Hale supported women's rights and education but was no suffragette, Lincoln stood against the spread of slavery but was no abolitionist. The editress from New Hampshire and the lawyer from Springfield had never met.

Like other publications, the *Lady's Book* was struggling as a result of the nation's hostilities. Just prior to the outset of the war, the magazine's circulation had reached its peak of 150,000 individual subscribers, with its pass-along readership far exceeding that number. The magazine was a hot commodity, making its way from parlor to parlor via eager readers who were not be able to afford a subscription of their own. Now the publication—which delivered its issues via everything from stagecoach to steamboat—lost a good deal of its subscribers when mail service between the northern and southern states came to an abrupt end, with no immediate solution on the horizon. The disruption curtailed readership as well as those ears sympathetic to Hale's causes— thanksgiving among them.

As battles sprung up in multiple states, Hale took to her magazine in 1861 to write of a bright spot on her own, hard-fought horizon, one close to her heart: the education of women. One of her passions was gaining a foothold on a national level. "While clouds and darkness overhang the land, we naturally welcome with double pleasure whatever promises permanent good for the future. The founding of an institution like Vassar Female College, in a year like the present, is a peculiarly cheering event," she noted.

When Hale had heard of brewer Matthew Vassar's intentions to open a college for women in Poughkeepsie, New York, she wrote him—early and then often—offering advice, making suggestions (welcome or not), and supporting his efforts however she could. She wrote about the school's developments almost obsessively in the pages of the *Lady's Book*. Vassar was to be the second institution in the United States to grant degrees of higher education to women that were on par with those granted at reputable men's colleges, following very closely behind Elmira College, also in New York State. However, when Hale later received word that the institution would not have women professors on the faculty, she took to the pages once again—to complain. Loudly. She made no bones about her displeasure and let Matthew Vassar know as well. She also took issue with the word *female* as a modifier in the institution's name—Vassar *Female* College. The word appalled her, and since the 1850s she had derided its use in the pages of *Godey's*. She likened the use of *female* when modifying human beings to the manner in which one might describe a farm animal. "What female do you mean?" she later wrote. "Not a female donkey?" She continued, "Then . . . why degrade the feminine sex to the level of animals." She soon implored Vassar to reconsider the institution's name, offering "Vassar College for Young Women" as an alternative, which she considered more "dignified." She ended her letter somewhat sternly: "Pray do not, my good friend, disappoint me."

Closer to home, Hale's passion for education had inspired her daughter Josepha to open a school for girls, which she ran from the Philadelphia home she shared with her editor mother. The pair had recently relocated to Rittenhouse Square, and the school along with it.

The Civil War presented other challenges and missed opportunities for Hale in her role as editor. The *Lady's Book*, with Louis Godey as its publisher, was already a decidedly *apolitical* magazine. It remained even more so with the country at war.

Godey—who typically granted Hale a tremendous amount of leeway and free rein in her role as editor—made no bones about keeping politics out of his publication. "I allow no man's religion to be attacked or sneered at, or the subject of politics to be mentioned in my magazine," Godey stated at a public dinner and later shared in his back-of-the-book column. "The first is obnoxious to myself and to the latter the ladies object; and it is my business and pleasure to please them, for to them—God bless the fairest portion of his creation—am I indebted for my success."

There were gentle, measured steps in Hale's editing of the magazine during the war. She took to the "Editors' Table" for an extensive, glowing overview of medical pioneer Florence Nightingale's book, *Notes on Nursing*. Hale enthusiastically encouraged her readers to buy the book and study it. "Her book is a wonderful monument of the power of truth when set forth by genius in the cause of humanity," she gushed. "This little volume of eighty pages is one of the most important works ever put forth by woman; and very few medical books, produced by the most eminent men, equal it in usefulness. . . ." However, the magazine missed other opportunities to rally its readership to the growing need for supplies, donations, and volunteers for organizations like the U.S. Sanitary Commission, a civilian-run aid organization (though recognized by the federal government) that lent a hand in hospitals and camps and raised money for food and supplies. The Sanitary Commission and its fundraising fairs, for example, were constantly seeking numbers to strengthen their ranks, and could have benefitted from repeated campaigning plugs in *Godey's*.

Hale's efforts on behalf of her favorite holiday continued, even as the prospect of "union" in the United States seemed ever more hopeless. In small ways, though, she allowed the context of the celebration to necessarily evolve to reflect the trying times. Following her praise of Nightingale in 1860, Hale shared with readers that 1859 had seen thirty states and three territories celebrate thanksgiving on the same day. "This year the last Thursday in November falls on the 29th," she wrote. "If all the States and Territories held their Thanksgiving on that day there will be a complete moral and social reunion of the *people* of America in 1860. Would not this be a good omen for the perpetual political union of the States? May God grant us not only the omen, but the fulfilment is our dearest wish!"

And again in 1861, Hale employed similar unifying language: "[A]midst all the agitations that stir the minds of men and cause the hearts of women to tremble . . . Shall we not, then, lay aside our enmities and strifes, and suspend our worldly cares, toils, and pursuits on *one day* in the year, devoting it to a public Thanksgiving for all the good gifts God has bestowed on us and on all the earth?" She continued, writing of the poor of other countries and the reasons her own nation had to be thankful. She encouraged her fellow citizens "to extend our sympathies beyond the limits of our own country," and wrote of "[p]eace on earth and good-will among men," adding that "All nations are members of one brotherhood. . . ."

There was certainly precedent for the holiday in even a divided land, including the South, and even beyond the congressional and presidential proclamations of the late eighteenth and early nineteenth centuries. Movement and migrations within the country had brought some Yankee traditions south, and the religious aspect of thanksgivings was familiar to many. Not twenty-five years prior to the start of the Civil War, Governor Charles Manly of North Carolina proclaimed Thursday the 15th of November "to be observed throughout this State as a day of general Thanksgiving." The proclamation stated that the General Assembly had directed the governor "for the time being . . . to set apart a day in every year, and to give notice thereof, by Proclamation, as a day of solemn and public thanksgiving . . . and I do recommend and earnestly desire that all secular employments may be suspended during the day." Georgia's governor had issued a similar proclamation in 1826. By the 1850s, Ohio was another state supporting Hale's contention that all states should give thanks on the same day each year.

And on June 13, 1861—shortly *after* the start of the war—clergyman Thomas Smyth preached at the First Presbyterian Church of Charleston, South Carolina, "on the day of National Fasting, Thanksgiving and Prayer." The title of his sermon was "The Battle of Fort Sumter: Its Mystery and Miracle: God's Mastery and Mercy."

In the fall of 1861, a national celebration was not to be. However, the following year, 1862, though thanksgiving was still not a *national* celebration, its observance by some at the state level would prove the day to be a fruitful one.

In Boston that November, Lewis Hayden and his wife, Harriet, invited Massachusetts governor John Albion Andrew to dine with them on thanksgiving. Hayden was a former slave and clothing store owner who now worked for the secretary of state's office. Governor Andrew, an abolitionist, was one of Hayden's dear friends. The large dinner gathering was at Hayden's home on what was then Southac Street in the city's Beacon Hill neighborhood. The home was also, thanks to Hayden, a station on the Underground Railroad. Hayden had a topic to broach with his friend that night: Might the president permit Black soldiers in the Union Army? Could Governor Andrew put forth the idea? Andrew told his friend that he would, indeed, ask for permission to form a regiment in his state for Black soldiers. Governor Andrew would also seek to find a spot among the Union forces for another remarkable abolitionist, one who had escaped slavery and then risked life and limb helping others do the same: Harriet Tubman.

As 1863 dawned and the war raged on, Hale wrote a New Year's editorial in which she hoped for a day that would throw "away the weapons of warfare and ensigns of military strife, so that influences of love and good-will may have room to work . . . [for] concord, prosperity and joy."

The year started auspiciously. In January 1863, Lincoln signed the Emancipation Proclamation. It stated that "all persons held as slaves within any State or designated part of a State, the people whereof shall then be in rebellion against the United States, shall be then, thenceforward, and forever free . . ." This did not free all enslaved people, but rather only those living in states that were rebelling against the Union. Enslaved individuals residing in "loyal" border states were not affected. George E. Fawcett composed "The President's Emancipation March" in honor of the occasion.

Immediately, the call went out seeking Black men to enlist. Governor Andrew had been true to his word. "I am about to raise a Colored Regiment in Massachusetts," Andrew wrote. "This I cannot but regard as perhaps the most important corps to be organized during the war." That thanksgiving dinner of 1862 had helped ensure the creation of the Massachusetts 54th Regiment.

"TO COLORED MEN!" read one such recruitment broadside. "FREEDOM, Protection, Pay, and a Call to Military Duty!"

Hayden helped recruit soldiers, and Frederick Douglass rallied the call as well. In spring of that year, the 54th Massachusetts Volunteer Infantry was off to war, consisting of 78 officers and 1,364 enlisted men. Frederick Douglass's sons Charles and Lewis were among the recruits, Lewis serving as the regiment's sergeant major. Charles would later transfer to the 5th Massachusetts Cavalry.

Also among those men was Corporal James Henry Gooding, who was a member of the New Bedford Company of the 54th.

"As the time draws near for the departure of the men . . . there is not a sufficient number to form a whole company," Gooding wrote. "Does it not behoove every colored man in this city to consider, rationally with himself, whether he cannot be one of the glorious 54th? Are the colored men here in New Bedford, who have the advantage of education, so blind to their own interest, in regard to their social development, that through fear of some double dealing, they will not now embrace probably the only opportunity that will ever be offered them to make themselves a people."

The next day the recruits marched through town, cheered on by a crowd and a band as they made their way to the train station. Upon assembling at city hall for roll call prior to departure, each recruit was given a pair of mittens. Governor Andrew of Massachusetts had also written General

David Hunter on behalf of Harriet Tubman. Hunter, a friend of Lincoln's and brother-in-law of Hale's daughter Frances, was eager to benefit from Tubman's knowledge and skill. Within months, Tubman—a Black woman and a civilian— would be instrumental in helping to conceive and execute a raid on the Combahee River in South Carolina. It was a first on numerous, previously inconceivable levels.

That spring brought another major personal loss for Hale: the passing of her daughter Josepha. Though her health had been suffering in recent years, Josepha's death at just forty-two years of age was unexpected. Though still grieving, come September 1863, Hale would, once again, publish her annual thanksgiving editorial. She called upon President Lincoln in the pages of her magazine, asking would it not be better if a "proclamation which appoints Thursday the 26th of November as the day of Thanksgiving for the people of the United States of America should, in the first instance, emanate from the President of the Republic—to be applied by the Governors of each and every State, in acquiescence with the chief executive adviser?" She was as committed as ever to her cause. Hope sprung eternal. Her pen would not rest.

Later that month, Hale penned the following letter. In the upper-left-hand corner of the missive, she wrote "private," underlining it for added effect. The letter was dated September 28, 1863, and addressed to "Hon. Abraham Lincoln— President of the United States."

Sir—

Permit me, as Editress of the "Lady's Book," to request a few minutes of your precious time while laying before you a subject of deep interest to myself and—as I trust—even to the President of our Republic of some importance. This subject is to have the <u>day of our annual Thanksgiving made a National and fixed Union Festival</u>.

You may have observed that, for some years now, there has been an increasing interest felt in our land to have the Thanksgiving held on the same day in all the States; it now needs <u>National</u> recognition and authoritative <u>fixation</u> only to become permanently an American custom and institution.

She enclosed clippings from magazines and newspapers to support her claim of the popularity of the idea.

For the last fifteen years I have set forth this idea in the "Lady's Book," and placed the paper before the governors of all the States and Territories—also I have sent these to our Ministers abroad and our Missionaries to the heathen and commanders in the Navy.

She described favorable and supportive responses from Governors but added, "I find there are obstacles not possible to be overcome without legislative aid," and that it should be "obligatory on the Governor to appoint the last Thursday of November, annually, as Thanksgiving Day."

She mentioned that she had also "written to my friend Hon. Wm. H. Seward," requesting he

> confer with President Lincoln on this subject, as the president of the United States has the power of appointments for the District of Columbia and the Territories, also for the Army and Navy and all American citizens abroad who claim protection from the U.S. flag—could he not with right as well as duty, issue his proclamation for a Day of National Thanksgiving for all the above classes of persons and would it not be fitting and patriotic for him to appeal to the Governors of all the States inviting and commending these to unite in issuing proclamations for the last Thursday in November as the Day of Thanksgiving for the people of each State? This the great Union Festival of America would be established.
>
> Now the purpose of this letter is to entreat President Lincoln to put forth his Proclamation, appointing the last Thursday in November (which falls this year on the 26th) as the National Thanksgiving for all those classes of people who are under the national Government particularly, and commending this Union Thanksgiving to each State Executive: thus, by the noble example and action of the President of the United States, the permanency

*and unity of our Great American Festival of
Thanksgiving would be forever secured.*

*An immediate proclamation would be necessary,
so as to reach all the States in season for State
appointments, also to anticipate the early
appointment by Governors.*

Excuse the liberty I have taken.

*With profound respect
Yours Truly
Sarah Josepha Hale,
Editress of the "Lady's Book"*

She included with her letter to Lincoln an article from
the *Lady's Book* that would run that very same month, September 1863:

*Would it not be of great advantage, socially,
nationally, religiously, to have the DAY of our
American Thanksgiving positively settled? Putting
aside the sectional feels and local incidents that
might be urged by any single State of isolated
Territory that desired to choose its own time, would
it not be more noble, more truly American, to
become nationally in unity when we offer to God
our tribute of joy and gratitude for the blessings of
the year?*

*Taking this view of the case, would it not be
better that the proclamation which appoints*

*Thursday the 26th of November (1863) as the day
of Thanksgiving for the people of the United States
of America should, in the first instance, emanate
from President of the Republic—to be applied by the
Governors of each and every State, in acquiescence
with the chief executive adviser?*

Hale sealed the letter and mailed it to Washington. What remained to be seen was how her latest request would be received, if at all.

She had lived through the term of every president yet of the United States, and the one now in the White House, President Abraham Lincoln, was the one whose attention she sought at a time when he had little to give.

Her first response came not from President Lincoln but rather from the secretary of state. Seward responded on September 29, 1863: "I have received your interesting letter . . . and have commended the same to the consideration of the president."

CHAPTER 7

OF TRAGEDY AND GRATITUDE

In preparation for what was required in the coming weeks, a certain amount of solace was needed. For Abraham Lincoln, there was often no better place than the Soldiers' Home, a mere three miles from the White House. While there, Lincoln stayed in the cottage. The word *cottage* was employed here more in the way it might be when speaking of a "cottage" in Newport, Rhode Island. Though the president's retreat was not as ornate as the palatial homes in that rarefied enclave, it was still quite substantial. Constructed in the Gothic Revival style, it boasted thirty-four rooms and had sweeping views of the capital.

George Riggs, a banker and the original owner of the home and surrounding three-hundred-acre estate, had sold it to the federal government just over ten years earlier, in 1851. In 1857, another building was added, also Gothic in style, and made available to retired soldiers. The institution had been called a military asylum up to that point. Lincoln was only the second president to abscond to this nearby retreat on a hill. Buchanan, Lincoln's predecessor, had stayed there as well, and had recommended the spot to his successor. Lincoln's first visit came just days after his inauguration.

In spring of 1863, the White House staff had packed up the family and their belongings and transferred them the short distance to a place that *felt* worlds away—but was still not far from the president's pressing responsibilities. Lincoln was not entirely alone on the grounds. More than one hundred veterans lived there, many of them immigrants who had fought for the United States in the War of 1812 and the Mexican-American War. Reminders of the current war populated Lincoln's rides into Washington, DC. His daily route on horseback took him along Rhode Island and Vermont Avenues, through refugee camps, and by the homes of residents. In addition to the people inhabiting the grounds at the Soldiers' Home, the institution's cemetery was visible from the very door of the Lincoln family cottage. Dozens of Civil War dead were now being buried there each day. The cemetery at Soldiers' Home was the first-ever nationally designated cemetery, and the only existing one at the time. The first-ever burial at Arlington National Cemetery would not occur until May 1864.

The prior year, Lincoln had spent June to November in the cottage, far from the often suffocating heat and humidity that hung over Washington, DC. At the time, he and his wife, Mary, were still reeling from the death of their young son William Wallace from what was believed to be typhoid fever, having lost him in February 1862. There had been little time to grieve. But at least there had been time for repose and space to think. It was here at the cottage that he had written the final draft of the Emancipation Proclamation in September 1862.

Now, in October 1863, Lincoln could look back at gains and losses, advances and retreats. But the pall of grief and death—no matter whether a battle had been won or lost—hung heavy over the nation after a particularly brutal battle that summer in Pennsylvania. It was to that solemn space that he would soon travel.

There were two pieces of writing yet to be issued in the president's name.

One much shorter than the other. Both destined to make a mark on the United States for decades to come.

As William H. Seward, Lincoln's secretary of state, would later recount, he had gone to see the president in late September; he found the man busy and alone in his office.

"They say, Mr. President," Seward began, "that we are stealing away the rights of the States."

The sovereignty of individual states to make their own legislative decisions regarding many issues—key among them slavery—had been a point of debate in America since the time of the colonies, and gained momentum during the debates surrounding the creation of the United States Constitution. It was a more contentious issue now.

"So I have come to-day to advise you," Seward continued, "that there is another State right I think we ought to steal."

"Well, Governor," Lincoln said, "what do you want to steal now?"

"The right to name Thanksgiving Day! We ought to have one national holiday, all over the country, instead of letting the Governors of States name half a dozen different days."

For his part, Lincoln felt that thanksgiving days themselves were based more in custom than rooted in any law. If governors could choose to proclaim a day of celebration, the president certainly could—and perhaps ought to. He was on board. Seward had already begun drafting a potential proclamation and shared what he had with Lincoln. Together the two polished it and quickly came to an agreement about its final form.

On October 3, 1863, exactly seventy-four years to the day George Washington issued his, President Abraham Lincoln issued the proclamation for a national day of Thanksgiving. Despite a year that had seen tremendous loss, Lincoln's proclamation began, and ended, on notes of sincere gratitude:

> The year that is drawing towards its close, has been filled with the blessings of fruitful fields and healthful skies. To these bounties, which are so constantly enjoyed that we are prone to forget the source from which they come, others have been added, which are of so extraordinary a nature, that they cannot fail to penetrate and soften even the heart which is habitually insensible to the ever watchful providence of Almighty God. In the midst of a civil war of unequaled

magnitude and severity, which has sometimes seemed to foreign States to invite and to provoke their aggression, peace has been preserved with all nations, order has been maintained, the laws have been respected and obeyed, and harmony has prevailed everywhere except in the theatre of military conflict; while that theatre has been greatly contracted by the advancing armies and navies of the Union. Needful diversions of wealth and of strength from the fields of peaceful industry to the national defense, have not arrested the plough, the shuttle or the ship; the axe has enlarged the borders of our settlements, and the mines, as well of iron and coal as of the precious metals, have yielded even more abundantly than heretofore. Population has steadily increased, notwithstanding the waste that has been made in the camp, the siege and the battle-field; and the country, rejoicing in the consciousness of augmented strength and vigor, is permitted to expect continuance of years with large increase of freedom.

No human counsel hath devised nor hath any mortal hand worked out these great things. They are the gracious gifts of the Most High God, who, while dealing with us in anger for our sins, hath nevertheless remembered mercy. It has seemed to me fit and proper that they should be solemnly, reverently and gratefully acknowledged as with one heart and one voice by the whole American People. I do therefore invite my fellow citizens in every part of the United States, and also those who are at sea and those who are sojourning in foreign lands, to set apart and observe the last Thursday of November next, as a day of Thanksgiving and Praise to our beneficent Father who dwelleth in the Heavens. And I recommend to them that while offering up the ascriptions justly due to Him for such singular deliverances and blessings, they do also, with humble penitence for our national perverseness and disobedience, commend to His tender care all those who have become widows, orphans, mourners or sufferers in the lamentable civil strife in which we are unavoidably engaged, and fervently implore the interposition of the Almighty Hand to heal the wounds of the nation and to restore it as soon as may be consistent with the Divine purposes to the full enjoyment of peace, harmony, tranquility and Union.

In testimony whereof, I have hereunto set my hand and caused the Seal of the United States to be affixed. Done at the City of Washington, this Third day of October, in the year of our Lord one thousand eight hundred and sixty-three, and of the Independence of the Unites States the Eighty-eighth.

By the President: Abraham Lincoln

William H. Seward, Secretary of State

The date chosen and suggested specifically by Hale in her letter to Lincoln and in the pages of the *Lady's Book* was Thursday, November 26—also seventy-four years to the day after Washington's day of National Thanksgiving. Could Washington have imagined that not one hundred years after his proclamation the nation he had seen come into being would be threatened from within its own borders by divisiveness and hatred? Nevertheless, Hale's tireless efforts, and Seward's receptive ear and fluid pen, resulted in a proclamation for unity and thanks at a time when few could imagine either.

It had been thirty-six years since Hale had first described her thanksgiving feast in the pages of her novel *Northwood*. For at least fifteen years in the pages of the *Lady's Book*, she had continually waxed lyrical about the virtues of her vision. After constant petitions to governors, territory magistrates, ministers overseas—and yes, now a fifth president—her goal was achieved. With neither pomp nor circumstance and little to no fanfare, the proclamation that Hale had long envisioned and worked to secure could finally be seen in writing. Her long-held dream was becoming a reality, presidentially stamped and broadcast via the nation's—and world's— newspapers.

The announcement of Lincoln's proclamation was in undeniable black and white, though the words could have easily been lost among the reports of souls lost in battle, dispatches from besieged front lines, and pleas for funds and support of a more urgent and desperate kind, as opposed to pleas for a time to give thanks for all that was good. Predictably, the news prompted different reactions. One Virginia newspaper mocked "King Abraham's" proclamation, while the issuance moved Episcopal clergyman and education advocate William Augustus Muhlenberg to write "The President's Hymn" in honor of the occasion:

> *Give thanks, all ye people, give thanks to the Lord,*
> *Alleluias of freedom, with joyful accord;*
> *Let the East and the West, North and South roll*
> *along,*
> *Sea, mountain and prairie, One thanksgiving Song.*

Whether other citizens throughout the North and South would join in Hale's enthusiasm for a national day of thanks come November remained to be seen. Considering the schismatic climate, this was definitely the biggest question. Still, now, in the midst of all that was most bleak in the world, there would be a bid to come together to say thank you.

Sarah Josepha Hale was seventy-five years old.

After years of presidents ignoring her requests, it must have seemed almost unbelievable, the *speed* with which Lincoln's office responded to Hale.

How was it that this president—this president in particular—of all those leaders to whom Hale had pled her case for grace, had the time or inclination to take her fictionalized feast of gratitude and transform it, by presidential proclamation, into a true day of observance? And could either Hale or the president have known that such a day, rooted in tradition and yet marred by controversy, would grow into a most popular of holidays for generations to come?

The proclamation itself spoke not only of thanks but also

of the hardships that had been and were continuing to be endured by all. In that juxtaposition, between the good and evil in the world, a little bit of light emerged from within the litany describing these darkest of times.

In the midst of discord—"of a civil war of unequaled magnitude and severity"—came a plea for unity. The "bounties" to which Lincoln's proclamation referred were to be "solemnly, reverently and gratefully acknowledged." And so, when a country seemed most divided, Lincoln may have sought a reason for people to come together, however briefly. If so, then Sarah Josepha Hale gave him that reason. It was an example of how the press and a president could work together to achieve a moment of unanimity despite harrowing circumstances and cultural and political differences. It was the tiniest glimpse of what America could be.

But the day of observance itself would come on the heels of a more somber occasion.

The words that Lincoln and Seward had committed to the record that October would far outnumber those that Lincoln would speak just over a month later. One occasion had little to do with the other, yet everything to do with how these moments would be connected in years to come. The president's later words would understandably outshine the proclamation itself. The latter words would set the stage for a coming day of thanks that would herald the virtue of gratitude in these cruel times.

Two days after Lincoln issued the Thanksgiving proclamation, on October 5, 1863, the Confederate ship *David* attacked the *New Ironsides* just outside Charleston Harbor. And so the war carried on. Lincoln and the family stayed at the cottage at Soldiers' Home through the end of that month, as the president worked on a speech that would be roughly half the length of his proclamation of gratitude. Despite its brevity, it would have an impact, both immediate and lasting, of which few—probably even Lincoln himself—could conceive.

Upon returning to Washington and the White House, Lincoln indulged in the occasional diversion, theater being a favorite outing. On November 9, he and Mary went to Ford's Theatre, where they sat down in their usual box to see *The Marble Heart*. Lincoln enjoyed the lead actor's performance so much that he sent a note backstage to the thespian, requesting an audience. The star of the show, John Wilkes Booth, did not respond.

Standing on the battlefield, there seemed little reason to be thankful. How many bodies had lain here, wrecked and bloodied, lungs heaving their last breaths into the air still tinged with smoke and suffering? So many final exhalations had come and gone with no one to hear them over the thuds of cannon fire, screams of anguish, and cries of defiance. The site was infused with suffering. No matter who had ultimately claimed victory in this battle, this earth was steeped in inconsolable loss.

It was Thursday, November 19, 1863. Four and a half months had passed since the battle, and now had come the time to dedicate this ground. The president walked to the speaker's platform and sat, waiting. He was not, despite his position as commander in chief, the primary speaker of the day. Nor was he the first. The crowd gathered at the dedication of the Soldiers National Cemetery in Gettysburg, Pennsylvania, waited to hear what these men would say, and possibly wondered what words could equal the solemnity of the day. The man from Illinois perhaps knew that. Words could never convey what had transpired here.

Lincoln and a party of nearly twenty—including Seward, Lincoln's valet William Johnson, personal secretary John Nicolay, and assistant secretary John Hay—had left from Washington to head to the dedication. Hay and Nicolay had been friends since they were boys and served together under Lincoln. Hay, for one, kept diaries of his experiences. Lincoln was not feeling particularly well . . . and had not yet finished his speech.

Upon the entourage's arrival at Gettysburg, Lincoln left for the home of a wealthy local judge and the organizer of the following day's event, David Wills. Hay and some of the others wandered the streets, following the sounds of music. Hay observed groups singing and drinking whiskey. Crowds caroused. Buglers blew their horns. The streets buzzed as the night wore on. As for Lincoln, he, too, was up and about into the wee hours, continuing to edit and tweak his address.

The next day, the group made its way out to the cemetery. The procession "formed itself in an orphanly sort of way," Hay wrote, "& moved out with very little help from anybody." More than four months had passed since the battle, but the land remained in disarray, littered with the rotting carcasses of horses and the vultures that fed upon them. Scavengers of the human kind gathered up errant belt buckles, scraps of clothing, canteens, and the like, and hawked them as souvenirs. Photographers captured it all.

Edward Everett, a former senator and secretary of state under Millard Fillmore, was the key speaker for the day. A noted orator, Everett was one to draw a crowd. He took his place and began to speak. Once Everett's two-hour discourse ended, President Abraham Lincoln stood and spoke for approximately two minutes.

Lincoln took ten sentences to speak of sacrifice and the impossibility of honoring the occasion. "We cannot dedicate, we cannot consecrate—we cannot hallow—this ground. The brave men, living and dead, who struggled here, have consecrated it far above our poor power to add or detract," he said.

The president's economy of language caught many off guard. "Is that all?" one reporter asked. It was.

Everett himself knew something monumental had happened on that field, saying to Lincoln, "My speech will soon be forgotten, yours never will be. How gladly would I exchange my hundred pages for your twenty lines."

The president was not having it. "We shall try not to talk about my address," he said. "I failed, I failed, and that is about all that can be said about it."

Lincoln's opinion seemed an outlying one. Writer Ralph Waldo Emerson would later comment: "His brief speech at Gettysburg will not easily be surpassed by words on any recorded occasion."

While John Hay admired Everett's oratorical skills, too, he said of Lincoln that he spoke "in a fine, free way, with more grace than is his wont, said his half dozen words of consecration, and the music wailed and we went home through crowded and cheering streets."

Exactly one week later, on Thursday, November 26, another occasion would be marked, a pause taken, and thanks given for the blessings—however few—that coexisted alongside those horrors.

To be thankful when the sun and rains favor the crops, when the family is healthy and united, when the mood is light and the burdens are few and easily borne. When besieged by death and suffering, and in the face of injustice and horrors, a glimmer of relief struggles to be seen through the gloom. How much darker the days must have seemed a week after the dedication at Gettysburg, how much more poignant a day of thanks in the throes of the Civil War, and how much more welcome at that moment, that touch of grace.

Of all the publications that either commended or criticized the proclamation, one was notably absent that October: the *Lady's Book*. The October 1863 issue was packed, to be sure, and featured both the October walking suit and wrap, the cordovan and the Lonjumeau jacket, and some exciting new styles for dress bodices or "corsages"—including a French corsage that cinched the waist with two delicate bows. This month's tune, "Autumn Schottische," was written and arranged for the piano for *Godey's Lady's Book* by "Emancipation March" composer George E. Fawcett. The clothing patterns featured in the monthly "Work

Department" included a cravate Marie Therese and a crochet purse.

As the magazine had been compiled for printing months earlier, there was no mention of the president's October declaration. But in its letters to the editress, the magazine did print a note that captured some of that spirit and optimism:

"My Dear Mrs. Hale: For us who believe in a Providence that out of present evil educes future good, it is delightful to look on the bright side of this war, as it has shown some of the best traits of womanhood."

CHAPTER 8

ON A THURSDAY IN NOVEMBER

She knelt with hands clasped, her eyes raised skyward, with a shield and sword lying on the floor beside her. A flag was draped over the altar before her, and on that altar was engraved a single word: *UNION*.

The woman was Columbia, the personification of the United States of America, namesake of the nation's capital. She occupied the central panel of the illustration, titled "Thanksgiving-Day."

The German-born illustrator Thomas Nast had created the illustration for the December 5, 1863, issue of *Harper's Weekly: A Journal of Civilization*. In addition to the central panel featuring Columbia, there were three inset panels above and three below. The top center space featured presidents Washington and Lincoln, kneeling across from each other—Washington on the battlefield, Lincoln resting his forearms on a chair—as if this latest thanksgiving was in homage to that of 1789. This thanksgiving was occurring on the very same day in the month of November that Washington himself had chosen. "Thanksgiving-Day, November 26, 1863" ran across the bottom of the page. Panels featuring the army and the navy flanked the presidents, while beneath the image of Columbia were panels titled "Town," "Country," and "Emancipation." The characters in the images were both known and anonymous, common and heroic. Familiar politicians and average citizens.

Nast's sketches were not limited to cartoon illustrations; there were also—in an era of extremely limited photography—drawings of battlefield scenes. These and other artworks were initially engraved on wood before being transferred to print for publication. Magazines like *Harper's* employed engravers who would take an illustrator's work and meticulously carve it into wood in reverse. In order to facilitate this process, Nast, a prolific and sought-after illustrator, occasionally drew his images *backward* directly onto wood blocks himself.

At the time, Columbia was a popular and perhaps the most common physical representation of the young nation. Though Uncle Sam—commonly linked with a New York State meat-packer named Samuel Wilson who supplied troops during the War of 1812—had appeared as a national mascot as early as the 1820s, his ubiquitous scowl and goatee had yet to take firm hold in the nation's consciousness. (Nast himself would accelerate that process when he depicted Uncle Sam in 1869.)

One of the earliest expressions of Columbia—a name derived from Latin for "lands of Columbus"—as a persona came courtesy of the pen of Phillis Wheatley, the first Black poet in the colonies to publish a book of verse: *Poems on Various Subjects, Religious and Moral*, released in September 1773. Born in West Africa's Senegambia region, Wheatley was enslaved as a child, sent to Boston, and purchased by John and Susanna Wheatley. The Wheatleys' daughter tutored Phillis, who published her first poem in a Rhode Island newspaper in 1767. But it was her poem "To His Excellency, George Washington," which she sent to Washington himself and which was eventually published in *Pennsylvania Magazine*, that captured the spirit of Columbia as no one had before.

*The goddess comes, she moves
   divinely fair,
Olive and laurel binds her
   golden hair:
Wherever shines this native of
   the skies,
Unnumber'd charms and
   recent graces rise.*

*Muse! bow propitious while
   my pen relates
How pour her armies through
   a thousand gates . . .*

*Shall I to Washington their
   praise recite? . . .*

*Proceed, great chief, with
   virtue on thy side,
Thy ev'ry action let the
   goddess guide.
A crown, a mansion, and a
   throne that shine,
With gold unfading,
   WASHINGTON! be thine.*

Upon receiving the poem, Washington—who at the time had recently been appointed commander in chief of the Continental Army—wrote to Wheatley, thanking her for the "polite notice of me, in the elegant Lines you enclosed." The letter is believed to be the only occasion when Washington—who personally held more than one hundred enslaved people, not including those held by his wife, Martha—corresponded with an enslaved person. Wheatley's "elegant lines" and "great poetical Talents," as Washington observed, were formative in the creation of and hastened the acceptance of the personification of Columbia, which countless others—Thomas Nast among them—would later exploit.

A week before Nast's illustration appeared, a very divided nation and those beyond its borders watched as this new national thanksgiving unfolded. After Lincoln's proclamation, various governors throughout the country, including some in the South, followed suit.

Throughout the warring states, on both sides of the Mason-Dixon line, stories of simple and joyful, somber and reflective celebrations were shared. The war, of course, had not ceased; and in the press, stories abounded about the Union victories at Chattanooga. In Virginia, Massachusetts troops of the 10th and 37th regiments prepared for a battle. "Those who were not too much exhausted made fires over which their 'Thanksgiving Dinner' of coffee and 'hard tack' was prepared. The most sumptuous repast could not have been more welcome."

Nurse Clara Barton had spent much of 1863 off the coast of South Carolina, often between Hilton Head and Morris Island, ministering to battle-worn soldiers in both locales. In November, Barton traveled to St. Helena Island, also in South Carolina, where she celebrated the day with the 7th Connecticut Regiment stationed there. For the soldiers, there were ten roasted pigs. Barton and the wives—many of whom had become friends of the nursing legend—enjoyed a turkey dinner. That night, Barton set off for home, traveling across the bay.

The Union soldiers camped on Morris Island would have a decidedly different thanksgiving. Brigadier General Quincy Gillmore's troops had long been encamped on the South Carolina isle, having survived the brutal Second Battle of Fort Wagner earlier that year. Among those fighting in that battle was the 54th Massachusetts Regiment—the first official all-Black regiment in the Union Army—under the leadership of a Massachusetts patrician, Colonel Robert Gould Shaw. Frederick Douglass's son Charles had taken ill and never left Massachusetts after joining up with the 54th. But Charles's brother Lewis, then a sergeant, was there. He had written to his fiancée, Amelia, of the horrors of the wretched battles he had already endured, on the eve of what would be the most devastating encounter yet for his regiment. "My Dear girl I hope again to see you. I must bid you farewell should I be killed," he had written in July. "Remember if I die I die in a good cause."

Barton had been on hand to help wounded soldiers, and Lewis Douglass was among those injured. There were massive losses—more than fifteen hundred soldiers had died, including Shaw. Confederate forces had abandoned Fort Wagner just over a month earlier. The remaining Union troops managed to pull together their holiday, and later shared this correspondence with the South Carolina newspaper the *New South*:

"Of course you do not suppose that we had turkey, roast-beef champaign [sic] and the like. No! we poor soldiers, who fight for the honor of the old flag—thirteen dollars per month!—here no such epicurean desert [*sic*]; nor are we permitted to dream of good dinners unless by special order from the commissariat department. Yesterday, however, we tickled our diaphragms with dead pig salted, an extra red herring, some venerable pickles and then washed it down with the most villanous water yet discovered on this desolate island."

African American troops throughout the war shared their experiences of the holiday as well. William P. Woodlin, a Black soldier present at the siege of Petersburg, Virginia, wrote in his diary on November 26:

"Thanksgiving day. A present of $100 made to the Reg which was laid out in apples, pies & coffee. Speeches by Gov. Cannon of Del. a gentle[man] from Eng[land] and some others."

Corporal James Henry Gooding of the Massachusetts 54th—the regiment which had been at least partially hatched at that thanksgiving dinner in Boston only a year earlier—shared his regiment's version of the celebration, spent on Morris Island, as bombardment of nearby Fort Sumter and Charleston continued.

He wrote that the day was "just cool and keen enough to make one feel that it was a genuine old New England Thanksgiving day, although it was not impregnated with the odor of pumpkin pies, plum puddings, and wine sauce, nor the savory roasts, boils and 'schews' familiar to the yankee homes of New England. But we made up the deficiency by the religious observance of the day in a very appropriate manner."

Gooding shared his reports from the field with the

Mercury newspaper out of New Bedford, Massachusetts. "Our correspondent," the editors of that publication wrote, "is a colored man belonging to this city. . . . He is a truthful and intelligent correspondent, and a good soldier."

After the religious service was completed, the rest of the day was devoted to eating and sports. "The officers of each company treated their men," Gooding wrote, "to cakes, oranges, apples, raisins, besides baker's bread, and butter. There were also games including sack races and blindfolded wheelbarrow competitions. Added to that," he reported, "we had a greased pole set up, with a pair of new pantaloons tied to the end, with $13 in the pocket for the lucky one who could get it, by climbing to the top."

Reflecting on the volunteer nature of their dangerous trials, Gooding wrote, "So you see the boys are all alive and full of fun; they don't intend to be lonesome or discouraged whether Uncle Sam pays them or not; in fact the day was kept up by the 54th with more spirit than by any other regiment on the island."

Also tending to the needs of Black soldiers was women's rights activist and abolitionist Sojourner Truth. Sixty-six-year-old Truth, who had been born into slavery as Isabella Baumfree, had emancipated herself before being legally freed by New York's Anti-Slavery Act. She went from door to door in Battle Creek, Michigan, collecting funds for the First Michigan Regiment of colored soldiers bivouacked in Detroit so that they might enjoy a thanksgiving dinner. Though she was successful in her efforts, they were not always well received. One man greeted Truth by hurling insults at her about her race, the war, and more. Truth asked him his name. "I am the only son of my mother," he said, to which Truth replied, "I am glad there are no more." She delivered the food herself to those troops at Camp Ward, to an enthusiastic reception that was covered in the Detroit newspapers, among them the *Advertiser and Tribune*. "Sojourner Truth, who carries not only a tongue of fire, but a heart of love," the paper reported, "was the bearer of these offerings." Truth also delivered a speech on the occasion, "glowing with patriotism, exhortation, and good wishes, which was responded to by rounds of enthusiastic cheers."

Charity shone throughout the country, especially in the capital region of Washington, DC, where many thanksgiving dinners were served at area hospitals. In Wheeling, West Virginia, contributions were solicited for the soldiers' fund. In Buffalo, New York, a call went out in the local newspaper to visit the "fatherless and the widow in their affliction." A Nashville convalescent camp, with the aid of the U.S. Sanitary Commission, held religious services and served dinner to roughly two thousand recovering soldiers.

There were parades and balls and simple sermons. Government and business offices remained closed. In other areas, the affair was decidedly more robust and raucous. The Meridian Hill House in Washington held a "Grand Shooting Match" that thanksgiving day and announced in the paper a "prize to be a live bear weighing 200 pounds. Distance to be 600 yards. Come one, come all."

The southern states were not absent from the thanksgiving festivities by any stretch, though throughout the Confederacy, expressions and interpretations varied: Charles Macbeth, mayor of Charleston, South Carolina, proclaimed

November 19—a full week before Lincoln's appointed date—as a day of "Thanksgiving and Prayer," citing a "deep sense of gratitude" that "our beloved and venerated city has been so far mercifully preserved from the destruction meditated against it by a barbarous and blood-thirsty foe."

The *Daily True Delta* out of New Orleans called thanksgiving day "festive," adding that "the whole population of the city, we venture to say, was very thankful that those who could not sport the turkey on the table could satisfy the demands of nature with less costly food."

A hearty sense of humor was not lacking in the pages of the *New South* newspaper of Port Royal, South Carolina. One correspondent offered the following rundown of a celebration he attended, writing: "Net results of the dinner, one good speech, five middling ones, eight decidedly dull ones, and the balance not to be mentioned in the Department under penalty of death. Casualties, one Correspondent with head greatly enlarged; several with marasmus in the pocket . . . the baskets of 'cold wittals' for the missionaries at Beaufort. I hope the representatives of the Northern Press will hereafter remember me in all public dinners in the Department."

The U.S. territories, too—many of which had long been on the receiving end of Sarah Josepha Hale's campaign—partook of the day. The governor of the Washington territory, William Pickering, implored residents to hold religious meetings. The U.S. Minister Resident of Honolulu, as a "representative of the United States Government in His Majesty's Kingdom," asked that those on the Hawaiian Islands observe a day of thanksgiving and prayer. An article in the

Pacific Commercial Advertiser quoted the minister in what seemed to be a direct reference to Hale's ongoing efforts: "In 1860, twenty States held this anniversary on the last Thursday of November," the minister said, "and prior to the opening of the rebellion, there was a general desire expressed by the most influential papers in various parts of the Union that it should be changed from a State to a National Anniversary." The article continued, capturing a sentiment not uncommon in so many of the papers of the day: "A civil war may seem to some to be an unfit period for national thanksgiving. But a glance at the history of the past two years will show us much for which Americans have reason to be grateful."

The *London Times*, Confederate-leaning newspapers happily reported, thought Lincoln's actions presumptuous, as there was little for which to be thankful, and questioned why Lincoln was "justified in pronouncing with certainty that his affairs on the 26th November will call for thanksgiving and not humiliation?"

In contrast to the *Times*'s take, however, was the *Leavenworth Bulletin* out of Kansas, which noted the novelty of Lincoln's proclamation and asserted that the circumstances made the holiday most appropriate: "We believe no President, except the present, has ever suggested a Thanksgiving Day, and doubtless he never would, had it not been for the extraordinary times in which we live. In times past the Governor of each State has selected the day, conformable to the wishes of the people; but there is at this time an appropriateness in the action of the president which commends itself to all."

And on the far reaches of the United States, Governor

Leland Stanford of the thirteen-year-old state of California observed, "[W]hile we deplore our condition as a nation, we have manifold reasons for offering up our united thanksgiving as a community."

Those engaged in business—especially those who trafficked in turkeys, geese, ducks, and chickens—seized this opportunity to call attention to their wares. Grocers posted ads like this one for Dow & Burkhardt's of Louisville, Kentucky: "THANKSGIVING IS COMING," communicating its offerings in poetry:

> *The good old times of ancient bliss draw nigh,*
> *When sires turn to youth and youth to pie—. . . .*
> *But after all our joys were incomplete*
> *Without the luscious pies made from*
>   *mince-meat. . . .*

The purveyors waxed ever deliciously on, rhyming "plump" with "venison rump," adding, "While cranberry sauce, with turkeys fat and young add greater relish for the epicurean tongue."

Sadly, however, upon reaching the last line of their advertisement, the writers were at a loss to find anything of the season's sale to rhyme with "Burkhardt's."

The feast day was not without incident, of course. California's *Santa Cruz Weekly* reported a theft at a local ranch of a dozen turkeys, all of which had been slated for thanksgiving celebrations throughout their community. "May the gaunt ghosts of twelve spoiled dinners haunt the villain," the paper wrote.

Meanwhile, across the ocean, the president and Hale's call for unity was embraced even in that first year. A correspondent for the *New York Times* reported on a thanksgiving celebration in Berlin, including services at the American Chapel and dinner at the St. Petersburg Hotel with many German guests in attendance. Ministers to Switzerland and Berlin raised toasts to Lincoln and the king and royal family of Prussia. Dr. Henry Philip Tappan, president of the University of Michigan, raised a glass to the Union—"it must and shall be preserved"—and the paper enthused that "[t]he cause of liberty throughout the world was inseparably connected with the perpetuity of the American Union." After singing the praises of prior meals and festivals enjoyed in the German city, the correspondent raved, "None, however, will be remembered longer or more pleasantly than that of the present year, which was much more numerously attended than its predecessors, and was held in observance of our first National Thanksgiving."

Sir: Among the many remarkable incidents of our recent Fair, not one has been more pleasant, than the duty that devolves upon us of consigning to you, on this National Thanksgiving Day, the accompanying watch."

This letter, written to Lincoln by the managers of the Northwestern Sanitary Fair, arrived from Chicago along with a gift: a gold watch. The timepiece had been donated to the fundraising cause as a reward for whoever was the largest contributor to the fair. "'Thou Art the Man,'" the letter continued. Lincoln had donated for auction a signed copy of the Emancipation Proclamation. "Your glorious Emancipation Proclamation, world wide in its interests and results, was sold for $3,000, the largest benefaction of any individual."

Yet for Lincoln, the day was not nearly as celebratory as it might have been.

"The president is sick in bed," John Hay noted in his diary on thanksgiving day. "Bilious." President Lincoln in fact had been struck down by varioloid, a mild form of smallpox. He was cared for by his African American valet, William Johnson, who remained at Lincoln's side throughout the ordeal.

Thanksgiving activities in Washington, DC, extended into the evening. "Ford's New Theater" announced in the newspaper that its location on Tenth Street would offer two performances on November 26, "in order to give a proper reception to the advent of the Thanksgiving festivities. . . . We have but one word of advice to those who design visiting Ford's on Thanksgiving Day, viz: secure seats early."

Home sick and bedridden, President Lincoln did not have plans to attend the broadly touted theater performances at Ford's. Not that night.

CHAPTER 9

REASONABLE HOPES

Ironically, the two people most directly involved in the national thanksgiving proclamation of 1863—Sarah Josepha Hale and Abraham Lincoln—were absent, at least in the public sense, from the activities that late November.

Hale was unable to provide comment in the November 1863 edition of the *Lady's Book* on what she surely must have regarded as a momentous and long-awaited event. The publication had already gone to press before Hale had received the good news from Washington. She would not weigh in on the matter until early 1864. Still, in keeping with publisher Louis Godey's well-known and oft-stated desire to keep the magazine as politics-free as possible, *printing* a presidential proclamation would likely have fallen outside the realm of possibility for the publication, even if it could have made the printing deadline. Hale appeared to allude to as much in an 1864 editorial titled "Our National Thanksgiving—a Domestic Festival," writing, "[I]n our endeavors . . . to secure the recognition of one day through-out the land as the Day of public Thanksgiving, we are con-scious of not having in any manner gone beyond the proper limits of the sphere which we have prescribed for the *Lady's Book*. It is the peculiar happiness of Thanksgiving Day that nothing political mingles in its observance."

Abraham Lincoln's first national thanksgiving came and went, with the president still abed. There he would remain through a good bit of December. Lincoln was eventually on the mend, but the situation in the feuding United States was not. Roughly a week after the holiday, on December 8, 1863, Lincoln issued the Proclamation of Amnesty and Recon-struction, turning an eye toward rebuilding the tattered na-tion once the war was finally over. However, for many that day still felt impossibly far off.

As Christmas approached, Lincoln was the recipient of an odd gift—a turkey. The president intended the bird for Christmas dinner, but young Tad Lincoln took a liking to it, naming him "Jack." On Christmas Eve, Tad got the bad news—Jack was destined for the table. Tad protested. Lin-coln gave in. He spared Jack the turkey, even putting the bird's stay of execution in writing: a presidential pardon.

Also on that Christmas Eve, Lincoln related a dream he had had the night before to his assistant secretary, John Hay.

"He was in a party of plain people," Hay wrote in his di-ary of his conversation with Lincoln, "and as it became known who he was, they began to comment on his appear-ance. One of them said, 'He is a very common-looking man.' The President replied, 'Common-looking people are the best in the world: that is the reason the Lord makes so many of them.' Waking," Hay wrote, "he remembered it, and told it as rather a neat thing."

As 1863 drew to a close, a third year of war loomed on the horizon. The "plain" and plainspoken man knew that soon there would be another political battle to wage: this one for his reelection. Recent years of national turmoil had not been kind to sitting presidents hoping for a second term. Once spring turned to summer, the Lincoln family again packed up their belongings and returned to the Soldiers' Home in order to escape the stifling seasonal heat and humidity of Washington. The president resumed his commute from the Soldiers' Home to the White House, and his rides through town from his summer residence to his office drew increased attention.

"I see the President almost every day," wrote the poet Walt Whitman, who inhabited a series of Washington, DC, boardinghouses during the war, "as I happen to live where he passes to or from his lodging out of town. I saw him this morning about 8 1/2 [8:30], coming in to business, riding on Vermont avenue, near L street." The writer's younger brother, George, had been wounded in 1862 at the Battle of Fredericksburg, and Whitman had promptly left his home in New York City—where he was known to frequent the same bohemian bar as illustrator Thomas Nast—to visit his brother in the hospital. Though his brother was only mildly injured, Whitman was unable to look away from the carnage he saw and volunteered as a nurse in various hospitals throughout Washington during the war. In addition to his own writing, Whitman described in his journals what he saw daily of the sick and dying. His reflections on Abraham Lincoln made their way onto Whitman's pages as well. "I see very plainly Abraham Lincoln's dark brown face, with the deep-cut lines," Whitman wrote, "the eyes, always to me with a deep latent sadness in the expressions. We have got so that we exchange bows, and very cordial ones."

On the seventh of July 1864, Lincoln issued another proclamation—this one calling for a day of national humiliation, fasting, and prayer. Both secular and religious in nature, the document spoke to faith, politics, and war. In it, Lincoln encouraged citizens to "convene at their usual places of worship," in hopes that, among other things, "those in rebellion . . . may lay down their arms and speedily return to their allegiance to the United States, that they may not be utterly destroyed, that the effusion of blood may be stayed, and that unity and fraternity may be restored and peace established throughout all our borders."

Of course, there was nothing quite like a predictable travel route to make matters simpler for anyone wishing the president ill. So very many did. Letters carrying death threats often arrived at the White House. Rumors proliferated that the president was to be kidnapped along his now well-known horseback commute. That year, while traveling back to the Soldiers' Home along his usual course, Lincoln was, as he wrote, "Immersed in deep thought, contemplating what was next to happen in the unsettled state of affairs," when he was fired upon. Luckily, the president's stovepipe hat took the brunt of the sniper's attempt. However, Lincoln's horse, Old Abe—"My erratic namesake," he wrote— did not take kindly to the gunshot, and "with one reckless bound he unceremoniously separated me from my eight-dollar plug-hat."

More obvious threats surrounded him as well. That summer of 1864 saw not only Union soldiers feeling hopeless but Lieutenant General Jubal Early and his Army of the Valley encroaching gradually but consistently on Washington, DC, raiding and looting as many Union cities, homes, and supply depots as they could. They were, in fact, encamped precariously close to the Soldiers' Home.

Around this time, Lincoln's oldest son, Robert Todd Lincoln, had completed his studies at Harvard University and taken a post as a staff officer for General Ulysses Grant, bringing the war even closer to home for the president. After losing two young children, Abraham and Mary Todd Lincoln now had a son at war. Tens of thousands of Union soldiers died over that summer, the number of bodies interred on the grounds of the Soldiers' Home only increasing beyond the door of Lincoln's summer residence.

Though Lincoln accepted the presidential nomination for the 1864 election, the incumbent was not confident of his success against Democratic nominee General George B. McClellan, who had served as Lincoln's head of the Army of the Potomac.

With elections looming and talk at the nominating convention of potential cease-fires and attempts to negotiate with the Confederacy on the lips of those in attendance, not to mention on the minds of those across the country, illustrator Thomas Nast again used his talents to comment on the national situation.

Compromise with the South—which happened to be the Democratic campaign slogan that year—was the title Nast chose for his latest illustration, which he dedicated to the Chicago Convention. Clearly capturing the feeling that any compromise with the Confederacy would essentially be experienced as defeat, Nast created a foreboding image depicting a triumphant Confederate soldier with his foot atop the grave of a Union soldier, its headstone reading "In Memory . . . Union Heroes in a Useless War." In the background, a Black Union soldier sits with his wife and child, all of them in shackles.

Fall approached. There was still no legal obligation for Lincoln to declare a national day of thanksgiving for the end of November. On October 9, 1864, Hale once again wrote to William H. Seward, reminding him of the upcoming anniversary of the previous year's thanksgiving day:

> *Enclosed is an article (or proof) on the National Thanksgiving. As you were, last year, kindly interested in this subject, I venture to request your good offices again. My article will appear in the November number of the "Lady's Book"; but before its publication I trust that* President Lincoln *will have issued his* proclamation appointing the last Thursday in November as the Day. *I send a copy of the* proof *for the President. You will greatly oblige me by handing this to him and acquainting him*

with the contents of this letter. I do not like to
trouble him with a note.

Hale hoped President Lincoln would issue the proclamation in time to alert Americans living outside the country as well: "[W]ould it not have a good effect on our citizens abroad? And if, on land and sea, wherever the American Flag floats over an American citizen all should be invited and unite in this National Thanksgiving, would it not be a glorious Festival?"

Later that October, Lincoln did, in fact, issue another presidential proclamation establishing a national day of thanksgiving, just as he had the previous October. It again set forth the same day: the last Thursday of November. This particular proclamation spoke of increasing the free population. It spoke of the enemy within our household. And again, it spoke of inestimable blessings. Proclamation number 118 was decidedly shorter than its predecessor, but it marked the first time that a successive proclamation of a national day of thanksgiving, on the same day of the same month, had ever been issued in the United States:

> It has pleased Almighty God to prolong our national life another year, defending us with his guardian care against unfriendly designs from abroad and vouchsafing to us in His mercy many and signal victories over the enemy, who is of our own household. It has also pleased our Heavenly Father to favor as well our citizens in their

homes as our soldiers in their camps and our sailors on the rivers and seas with unusual health. He has largely augmented our free population by emancipation and by immigration, while he has opened to us new sources of wealth and has crowned the labor of our working men in every department of industry with abundant rewards. Moreover, He has been pleased to animate and inspire our minds and hearts with fortitude, courage and resolution sufficient for the great trial of civil war into which we have been brought by our adherence as a nation to the cause of Freedom and Humanity, and to afford to us reasonable hopes of an ultimate and happy deliverance from all our dangers and afflictions.

Now, therefore, I, Abraham Lincoln, President of the United States, do, hereby, appoint and set apart the last Thursday in November next as a day, which I desire to be observed by all my fellow-citizens, wherever they may then be as a day of Thanksgiving and Praise to Almighty God, the beneficent Creator and Ruler of the Universe. And I do further recommend to my fellow-citizens aforesaid that on that occasion they do reverently humble themselves in the dust and from thence offer up penitent and fervent prayers and supplications to the Great Disposer of events for a return of the inestimable blessings of Peace, Union and Harmony throughout the land, which it has pleased him to assign as a dwelling place for ourselves and for our posterity throughout all generations.

In testimony whereof, I have hereunto set my hand and caused the seal of the United States to be affixed.

—Done at the city of Washington, this twentieth day of October, in the year of our Lord one thousand eight hundred and sixty four, and, of the Independence of the United States the eighty-ninth.

Ever the optimist, seventy-six-year-old Sarah Hale did not want to miss the opportunity to share this delightful news with her readership, no matter when the magazine had to go to press: "On the twenty-fourth of this month recurs the Day—'The last Thursday in November'—which has now become firmly established as one of the three National Festivals of America," she wrote in the November issue, referring to the longer-standing holidays of Washington's Birthday and Independence Day. She envisioned the celebration as a day "which lifts our hearts to Heaven in grateful devotion." She added that "the women of our country should take this day under their peculiar charge, and sanctify it to acts of piety, charity, and domestic love." Hale encouraged her readers to reach out to those less fortunate. "Let us each see to it that on *this one day* there shall be no family or individual, within the compass of our means to help, who shall not have some portion prepared, and some reason to join in the general Thanksgiving."

She also took the opportunity to recap her own progress

over the years, citing those who participated on a state-by-territory basis in 1859, 1860, and so on. In employing language such as "last Thursday in November" or "firmly established," *"fixed day"* or "yearly," Hale almost seemed to be working to convince her readers—if not perhaps even herself—that this time the proclamation would take hold for years to come, and that the holiday might be set for all time. Calling the day "fixed" and "annual" after just two consecutive years of proclamations may have been overly confident on her part, especially considering that the fate of the war had yet to be decided. Without an act of Congress, the holiday, its timing, and its celebration would forever remain at the whim of presidents, first and foremost, then governors. After decades of work and dreaming of this day, Hale was nothing if not tirelessly rosy and bullish.

As for President Lincoln, he again may have worried that come November there would not be much to be thankful for, this time because of the election. But Lincoln and his new running mate, Andrew Johnson, of the National Union Party—a temporary Civil War handle for the Republican Party—need not have worried. They won handily.

Several days before the holiday in 1864, Lincoln received a letter from a Providence, Rhode Island, man:

"Sir," the letter began,

> *I have taken the liberty of forwarding to you by*
> *Adams Ex. Co. two R.I. Turkeys for your*
> *Thanksgiving Dinner. They are "Narragansett"*

Turkeys celebrated in the New England and New
York markets as being the best in the world.
  Congratulating you up on the recent Election
I am

  Your obt. Svt
  Walter C. Simmons

Thomas Nast again took to the pages of *Harper's Weekly*
to create a thanksgiving illustration for readers. As the years
passed, Nast would depict the November holiday differently, often responding to the mood of the country as he
himself saw it. And with that approach, the tone of his ar-
tistic works might range from egalitarian hopefulness to hi-
erarchical exclusionism.

Nast's *Harper's Weekly* portrayal of that 1864 thanksgiving once again featured multiple panels. This illustration
stood in contrast to the downtrodden, foreboding nature of
Compromise with the South. In this new engraving, President Lincoln takes his place front and center, standing atop
the Confederate flag. Columbia is once again at an altar,
shield and sword ever by her side, with the legend reading,
"Thank God for Our Union Victories." The lower right of
the engraving featured a panel titled "On Board," which depicted sailors aboard a ship preparing to eat turkey. Similarly, the panel on the lower left, titled "In the Field," portrayed
soldiers seated on the ground of their camp and carving their
own bird. Thanks, too, was given to Maryland in one of the
panels for freeing its enslaved people. In the bottom center
of the illustration Nast included a panel titled "Blessed Be

the Peacemakers," featuring a group of generals poring over maps. The vision as a whole is one of both conflict and aspiration, hope and loss, and captured the thanksgivings that this country had experienced and perhaps what Lincoln wished to convey in proclaiming the holiday. Times are dire. And yet, thankfulness begins to tear at the dark shroud of despair, allowing in at least a little light.

Reports of how citizens celebrated that thanksgiving of 1864 were numerous, and included extensive acts of charity. The *Chicago Tribune* reported on November 23 that arrangements were being made for turkey to be served in the hospitals of Richmond, Virginia.

Tennessee's *Nashville Daily Union* pled for remembering those less fortunate: "And while in thousands of homes the day will pass with mirth and pleasure, we hope those who are suffering will not be forgotten. The consciousness of kind deeds performed, of hearts made glad, will add a keen relish to all the pleasures of the day, and like a benison of peace hover over the record of life's deeds. Let some concerted action upon this matter be taken and the day will then be made a Thanksgiving day indeed."

The *New York Herald* reported extensively on the content of sermons preached throughout the city, as well as festive and philanthropic activities. In Brooklyn, the American Temperance League treated the local newsboys to a dinner of turkey, roast beef, boiled cabbage, potatoes, pies, cakes, and fruits.

In Washington, DC, the temperature was fall at its best— cool and crisp but not oppressively cold. A local Sunday

school had helped raise money for the thanksgiving celebration held for those recovering at the Armory Square
Hospital.

Beyond the states themselves, the territories continued
the tradition as well, with the *Gold Hill Daily News* of the
Nevada Territory assuring readers that the "croppings at the
San Francisco Restaurant are rich and give promise of a layout worthy of the occasion. Turkey feathers are knee-deep
on the premises."

In the southern states, observances varied, with only
some governors following Lincoln's lead. Confederate president Jefferson Davis issued his own proclamation, declaring
November 16 as a day of thanksgiving throughout the *Confederate* states. Davis may not have wanted to join in with the
North, but he—as did so many others—still perhaps valued
what a day of thanks could mean.

The day before Davis's thanksgiving, on November 15,
the Confederate-friendly *Yorkville Enquirer* in South Carolina included the following suggestion among their news
items: "A movement is on foot in New York, to send 50,000
turkeys and 50,000 barrels of apples to Grant's army for a
thanksgiving dinner. Can't Gen. Hampton borrow a portion
of them for the use of General Lee's boys?"

Yet even if not celebrated, the day of November 24
brought some respite to the Confederate forces as well.

"Yesterday was observed as a day of thanksgiving in
Grant's army," the *Daily Dispatch* out of Richmond, Virginia, reported, "who, no doubt, devoured the several thousand turkeys sent them from the North. . . . There was

unbroken quiet all along the lines throughout the day. Even General Graham, commanding at Bermuda Hundred, finding it impossible to dislodge General Pickett from the advanced position captured by him last night a week ago, seems to have come to the conclusion to let him alone."

And from Petersburg, Virginia, one southern soldier reported, "The enemy observes this as thanksgiving day. All quiet." On that day, some bitter enemies chose to take a moment, no matter their passions or patriotic stances.

The quiet was short-lived, as fields returned to becoming battlefields and Major General William Tecumseh Sherman, marching to the sea, blazed a Union path of destruction along the way.

Come Christmastime, President Lincoln received a telegraph with an altogether different sort of gift:

> *I beg to present you as a Christmas gift the City of Savannah with 150 heavy guns & plenty of ammunition & also about 25,000 bales of cotton.*
>
> *W. T. Sherman*
> *Major Genl*

With increasing devastation in the South, war, if not division, if not loss, felt closer to an end.

CHAPTER 10

A TRADITION IN QUESTION

Acrowd of roughly seventeen hundred were on hand to watch the sold-out evening's show. *Our American Cousin* had already enjoyed nearly five hundred performances at London's Haymarket Theatre. Now it was showing in Washington, DC, at Ford's Theatre. Among those in the audience was twenty-three-year-old doctor Charles Leale, who had received his medical degree six weeks earlier and was now working at the U.S. Army General Hospital in Washington's Armory Square, as surgeon in charge of the wounded commissioned officers' ward. He was enjoying a well-deserved night off.

It was April 14, 1865. Leale took his seat in the theater. President Lincoln attended that Good Friday performance with his wife, Mary; Major Henry Rathbone; and Rathbone's fiancée, Clara Harris. The president and his entourage entered to cheers. The Lincolns bowed and took their seats. The mood was lighter than it had been for years. The war was over.

Losses and blockades had taken their toll early in 1865, and more and more Confederate troops had begun deserting. Though not yet ratified, the Thirteenth Amendment to the United States Constitution had passed the Senate in April 1864 and the House on January 31, 1865; Senate members represented states in the North; border states that did not leave the Union; and two new states, West Virginia and Nevada. "Neither slavery nor involuntary servitude, except as a punishment for crime whereof the party shall have been duly convicted, shall exist within the United States, or any place subject to their jurisdiction." The amendment still needed to be ratified in order for it to go into effect. The prior spring, in March 1864, General Ulysses S. Grant had been appointed general in chief of the Army—the first person ever to hold that post in the United States—giving him command of the nation's entire military.

Grant's military secretary, Ely S. Parker, was a diplomat, engineer, attorney, and a citizen of the Tonawanda Seneca Nation. The pair had known each other since 1860, when Parker frequented a store run by Grant's father and where Grant, who at that time had drunk himself temporarily out of his military career, was working. By 1863 and the Battle of Vicksburg, Grant had turned his life and career around. When Parker was denied the opportunity to enlist in the Union Army, he contacted Grant, who agreed to take him on personally. In April 1865, Richmond, capital of the Confederate States of America, fell. On April 9, 1865, in front of the Appomattox courthouse, generals Grant and Lee agreed upon the terms of Lee's surrender. Ely Parker wrote those terms.

At the close of the Civil War, the estimation of the death toll exceeded six hundred thousand souls. About twenty thousand each Hispanic and Indigenous peoples fought in Union and Confederate armies. In places like North Carolina and Virginia, members of the Pamunkey and Lumbee tribes served as naval pilots and guerrillas. Pequot fought in the 31st U.S. Colored Infantry, while Company K of the 1st Michigan Sharpshooters comprised Delaware, Huron, Oneida, Potawatomi, Ojibwa, and Ottawa. An estimated 198,000 Black men served in the U.S. Army and Navy, with roughly 40,000 of them losing their lives. And some who fought defied many challenges and prejudices, namely Harriet Tubman, who nursed, scouted, and spied in the South.

The country, including its beleaguered president, was anxious to move in a more peaceful direction, though the path and the scope of the reconstruction seemed unclear. Everyone wanted a chance to exhale, be with those who were home safe, mourn those who never would return.

Shortly after Lee's surrender, on April 11, Lincoln gave an address from the balcony of the executive mansion. Lately the president had been uneasy, troubled by disturbing dreams. He was subdued. The gathered crowd was not. Cheers erupted at the sight of him.

"We meet this evening, not in sorrow, but in gladness of heart," he began. He acknowledged the road ahead was "fraught with great difficulty." The president also promised to proclaim a day of national thanksgiving for the end of the war. Lincoln spoke a great deal to the issue of reconstruction; in particular, he addressed the state of affairs in Louisiana, which had formed a new state government that pledged loyalty to the Union. Not everyone in the throng found the president's words encouraging. Among those present was the actor John Wilkes Booth, who bristled with rage when Lincoln, still discussing Louisiana's constituency, said he favored extending the right to vote to Black men, specifically the "very intelligent" and "those who serve our cause as soldiers." Booth feared this would bring men of color one step closer to fully realized citizenship. "Now, by God I'll put him through," Booth said to his companions, Lewis Powell and David Herold. "That is the last speech he'll ever make."

Dr. Leale, too, had seen Lincoln's address days earlier. He had heard the president would be at Ford's the coming Friday, and decided to attend the theater the very same night. London's literary periodical *Athenaeum* and other publications had praised the three-act English farce about an American traveling to England on family business, during its London run. Act 3, scene 2, in particular, almost always offered a guaranteed laugh. One actor in the theater that night decided to make the most of that scene. That actor, though he had tread those boards in times past, was not on the stage that evening. He did, however, know the building's layout intimately.

Leale watched. The scene unfolded. The crowd laughed, as did the president. Then the sound of a gunshot caught Leale's ear. He turned toward the sound and saw a man leaping to the stage, his foot catching in the American flag that hung from the front of Lincoln's box. Dr. Leale rose from his seat and dashed in the direction of the president.

"O Doctor," Mary Todd Lincoln cried, "do what you can for him, do what you can!"

Leale stooped near the president's wife. She was to his right, holding Lincoln's head and sobbing. Major Rathbone, too, was injured. When Rathbone had attempted to apprehend the assassin, John Wilkes Booth, Booth had slashed Rathbone's left arm with a dagger. Dr. Leale demanded brandy and water.

Leale described finding the president in a "profoundly comatose condition," adding "his breathing was intermittent and exceedingly stertorous." Leale put his finger to Lincoln's right wrist. No sign of a pulse. He held Lincoln's head and shoulders, and two men helped him lay the president down on the floor of the theater box. They cut the coat and shirt off the president's body, seeking the source of the blood they felt, yet no shoulder wound was found. While examining the back of Lincoln's head, Leale found a clot of blood near the base of the skull. He inserted the little finger of his left hand through the smooth opening, where the bullet had entered Lincoln's brain. "As soon as I removed my finger a slight oozing of blood followed and his breathing became more regular," Leale later wrote.

Doctors Charles Taft and Albert King arrived and advised moving the president to a nearby house. Rathbone and Miss Harris joined them, the bloodied and injured Rathbone escorting Mary Todd Lincoln to the Petersen boardinghouse across the now-crowded street. The president's personal physician, Dr. Robert Stone, arrived, as did Surgeon General

Joseph Barnes and Assistant Surgeon General Charles Crane. Becoming increasingly apoplectic, Mary was forcibly removed to another room. They were eventually joined by Lincoln's son Captain Robert Todd Lincoln, who stayed by his father's side for most of the night, when not consoling his mother. At 7:20 a.m., Lincoln "breathed his last and 'the spirit fled to God who gave it,'" Leale wrote in a report, paraphrasing Ecclesiastes. All those there bowed and "supplicated to God in behalf of the bereaved family and our afflicted country."

Throughout his presidency, Lincoln had received death threats, both vague and specific, ominous and strange. The sniper attack on horseback. Rumors of a kidnapping. Two such letters from his first year in office capture some of the animosity and hatred that marred Lincoln's presidency and ultimately claimed his life:

[1861]

Abraham Lincoln Esq

Sir
     You will be shot on the 4th of March 1861 by a Louisiana Creole we are decided and our aim is sure.

     A young creole.
     BEWARE

February 20, 1861

Mr. Lincoln—
   May the hand of the devil strike you down
before long—You are destroying the country
Damn you—every breath you take—

Hand of God against you

These threats and many others may have proved futile, but John Wilkes Booth and his .44-caliber derringer pistol had succeeded where others had not. Abraham Lincoln was dead, the sixteenth president of the United States and the first to be assassinated.

Vice President Andrew Johnson had left the Petersen House and returned to his residence at the Kirkwood House at Twelfth Street and Pennsylvania Avenue NW, where he would prepare for the next, unexpected stage of his career. He was not aware that an attempt on his life had also been planned, but his would-be assassin had gotten cold feet and abandoned his mission. Seward was not so lucky. Lewis Powell, Booth's associate, broke into Seward's home and fought with members of his family and staff, stabbing six individuals before attacking Seward himself, who was in bed recovering from a carriage accident. Striking Seward about the face and neck did not prove fatal, however, as Seward's neck splint was ultimately an adequate deterrent to Powell's knife.

It had been not quite a month and a half since Johnson

had been sworn in as vice president—an event at which he was notoriously and quite noticeably drunk. This occasion was far more sobering. At 10 a.m., the hour had arrived. Chief Justice Salmon P. Chase arrived to perform the duties. Ironically, the Bible upon which Johnson swore his oath of office was open to Proverbs 20 and 21, the first of which states, "Wine is a mocker, strong drink *is* raging: and whosoever is deceived thereby is not wise." Nevertheless, Andrew Johnson took his oath to become the seventeenth president of the United States of America.

Johnson's first presidential proclamation arrived on April 25, 1865, setting aside May 25 as a "Day of Fasting, Humiliation and Mourning" for Lincoln's death.

"In memory," he wrote, "of the good man who has been removed."

And mourn the nation did. Homage was paid in a variety of manners, some in the form of poetry, some by the pen of poet Walt Whitman, who had written many poems about the emerging identity of America, and Lincoln in particular. During his tenure as a nurse in the Washington, DC, area, Whitman had witnessed much in the way of the human experience that had both distressed and inspired him. The last moments of a young soldier's life. An unexpected mercy. Fleeting glimpses of the president on his way to and from his duties at the White House.

President Lincoln was not sitting atop Old Abe for this trip through town. The last time anyone would have occasion to espy the sixteenth president of the United States making his way through the streets of the nation's capital, it would not be his person they would hail, but rather the procession, or the train that would carry Abraham Lincoln, one last time, to his home state of Illinois. Lincoln's remains made this final journey along with those of young William Lincoln, who had died three years earlier. Lincoln's most trusted valet, a Black man named William Slade, had prepared the president's body for burial. Whitman's words never rang truer:

> O Captain! my Captain! our fearful trip is done;
> The ship has weather'd every rack, the prize we
>   sought is won;
> The port is near, the bells I hear, the people all
>   exulting,
> While follow eyes the steady keel, the vessel grim
>   and daring:
> But O heart! heart! heart!
> Leave you not the little spot,
> Where on the deck my captain lies,
> Fallen cold and dead.

And this time Nast's Columbia wept. Her eyes showed no glimmer of hope. Her face was not raised in praise or valor, but rather buried in her hand. Her shield was nowhere to be seen. The American flag upon which she rested her outstretched arm lay draped over a casket.

Lincoln did not live to see the ratification of the Thirteenth Amendment in December 1865. Several months earlier, in August, Frederick Douglass wrote Mary Todd Lincoln from his home in Rochester, New York, to thank her for a gift: the president's favorite walking stick.

"I assure you," Douglass wrote, "that this inestimable memento of his Excellency will be retained in my possession while I live—an object of sacred interest—a token not merely of the kind consideration in which I have reason to know that the President was pleased to hold me personally, but as an indication of his humane interest [in the] welfare of my whole race."

In June, the *Lady's Book* printed a simple message:

We Mourn! Our Chief has Fallen!
ABRAHAM LINCOLN IS DEAD!

In the months after Lincoln's death, Hale pondered her own mortality. At the end of May, she sat down to write her last will and testament.

Whether Hale's legacy weighed heavier on her mind considering recent events can't be confirmed, but that very legacy, with or without her attention, was taking on a life of its own.

As the sadness of spring passed and fall approached once again, Vassar Female College opened its doors to more than 350 young women, which cheered Hale immensely. Even more encouraging—and thanks in no small part to Hale's persistence—twenty-four of the professors were also women. Within a year, the trustees would agree to remove "female" from the school's name and would soon remove that word from the marble facade of the campus's main building.

But her dearest campaign was never far from her thoughts. Hale's determination to create a national holiday had not been swayed by recent events. She saw no reason not to continue to petition yet another president to continue with what she had already proclaimed was an established annual tradition.

As she had so many times before, Hale appealed to her readers to rescue the popularity of the holiday. In November 1865, the "Editors' Table" of the *Lady's Book* was titled "Our National Thanksgiving Day. The Pledge of American Union Forever."

"Our Thanksgiving Day becoming the focus, as it were, of the private life and virtues of the people, should be hallowed and exalted, and made the day of generous deeds and innocent enjoyments, of noble aspirations and heavenly hopes," Hale wrote. She then launched into her own story. "Nineteen years ago the idea of this united American Thanksgiving Day was put forth by the Editress of the Lady's Book. . . . Our late beloved and lamented President Lincoln recognized the truth of these ideas as soon as they were presented to him. . . . But at that time, and also in November, 1864, he was not able to influence the States in rebellion, so that the festival was, necessarily, incomplete. President Johnson," she continued, "has a happier lot. His voice can reach all American citizens." Hale continued her public plea by stating, "The 30th of November, 1865, will bring the consummation."

Despite Hale's confidence, the thirtieth did not bring that consummation. On October 28, 1865, Johnson issued the third consecutive presidential proclamation for a national day of thanksgiving in the United States—but not for the last Thursday of November. Instead, he chose December 7, writing:

> **Whereas it has pleased Almighty God during the year which is now coming to an end to relieve our beloved country from the fearful scourge of civil war and to permit us to secure the blessings of peace, unity, and harmony, with a great enlargement of civil liberty; and**
>
> **Whereas our Heavenly Father has also during the year graciously averted from us the calamities of foreign war, pestilence, and famine, while our granaries are full of the fruits of an abundant season.**

Hale's incorrect prediction of the *date* notwithstanding, the holiday enjoyed wider observance in the newly unified country. Southern newspapers carried the news of the holiday, including the editors of the *Daily Progress* of Raleigh, North Carolina, who wrote, "we do trust that our whole people will show a proper regard for the day with an entire suspension of business and proper religious exercises on the occasion." Four days later, *The Daily Standard* of that same city reported: "Thanksgiving day was generally observed throughout the country." In Charleston, the *South Carolina Leader* reported on services held at the Zion Presbyterian

Church, writing: "All seemed to feel the same gratitude for the blessings bestowed upon us. . . . Our pen will not do justice to the occasion, and we can only say that it was the best meeting we ever attended. It was a real old-fashioned New England Thanksgiving, only more so."

Thomas Nast's illustration that first year after the close of the Civil War focused on peace, unity, an abundance of industrious acts and fruitful crops, and soldiers returning home from battle. The central panel featured a well-attended, if somewhat somber, thanksgiving meal. There was much reason, it seemed, despite the nation's losses, for gratitude, but the scene fell appropriately short of evoking an air of celebration. The day before the observance carried even more import that year, as Georgia became the twenty-seventh state to ratify the Thirteenth Amendment. It was official: Slavery in the United States was no more.

Johnson's administration would go down in history as one of the least successful ever. He was impeached by the House for violating the Tenure of Office Act when he removed Secretary of War Edwin Stanton from his cabinet. Acquitted by the Senate, Johnson ultimately survived his impeachment process by one vote and slid toward the finish line as a one-term president who had followed in the footsteps of a giant. While in office, he kept the thanksgiving tradition going by issuing three more proclamations, calling for thanks in 1866 for an "indispensable condition of peace, security and progress," as well as many "peculiar blessings." Johnson noted that the civil "war that so recently closed among us has not been anywhere reopened," and spoke of fields that "have yielded quite abundantly" the success of the mining industry, the resuming of commerce abroad, and the extension of the railroads.

Then, in October 1867, Johnson's proclamation started out differently than prior ones made by him or, for that matter, Abraham Lincoln or George Washington. Rather than starting with a list of things for which to be thankful, he instead seemed to acknowledge Hale's desire for the holiday to be a permanent fixture on the American calendar. His proclamation that year spoke directly to the seeds of the tradition:

"In conformity with a recent custom that may now be regarded as established on national consent and approval, I, Andrew Johnson, President of the United States, do hereby recommend to my fellow-citizens that Thursday, the 28th of November next, be set apart and observed throughout the Republic as a day of national thanksgiving and praise." He then marched through the now-expected litany of "abundant harvests" and prosperous industries "in our workshops, in our mines, and in our forests," and spoke of the extension of "iron roads."

As Washington and Lincoln had, Johnson crossed Thomas Jefferson's no-man's-land—the separation of church and state—and ascribed the nation's blessing to the divine: "He has inclined our hearts to turn away from domestic contentions and commotions consequent upon a distracting and desolating civil war, and to walk more and more in the ancient ways of loyalty, conciliation, and brotherly love."

Now in her seventy-ninth year, it would seem Hale still

could not rest. With an annual thanksgiving established amid such divisiveness and discord, the question now remained how, if at all, it might survive without Hale herself.

The *Lady's Book* survived the war intact, though subscriptions had taken a hit, falling to roughly 110,000. However, four years later, in January 1869, Louis Godey boasted that the magazine's readership was up to 500,000 subscribers— perhaps employing his own special "readership math," which included those who perused, but did not buy, the publication. That same month, the magazine reviewed the work of yet another up-and-coming woman writer. "Miss Alcott's reputation as a writer of 'juveniles' is here well sustained," Hale wrote of Louisa May Alcott's book *Little Women*. "The story is easy, natural, and interesting. We know of no better present for the holidays." Letting no moss grow under her own literary footing, Hale had published yet another book of her own, this one titled, aptly, *Manners; or, Happy Homes and Good Society All the Year Round*. Hale dedicated the book: "To young people particularly, and to all who seek happiness in this life, or for the hope of happiness in the life to come, this book is offered as a friend in their pursuits." Within that book of domestic advice a chapter is titled: "Our National Thanksgiving Day." In it, Hale detailed the journey to Lincoln's proclamation and continued to press the need for the official establishment of the holiday, expressing gladness that "this has already been done in a measure."

She continued, "There is something peculiarly beautiful

in seeing a great people, of the most varying creeds and opinions, bound by no established faith, thus voluntarily uniting throughout our wide land to mingle their voices in one common hymn of praise and thanksgiving."

In February 1869, those thousands of subscribers read of the success of the prior year's festivities, which Hale described in detail, delighting in surveying celebrations not only throughout "the Republic" but also in Alaska—"the first Thanksgiving day ever known in that boreal region"—as well as in Paris, Rome, and Berlin. She lauded the presence of "traditional roast turkey" on tables in Japan, Russia, and Brazil.

She then made a public plea of sorts. Perhaps as a nudge to the incoming president. Perhaps as a reaction to President Johnson's designating the 1865 holiday in December, rather than on the last Thursday in November. Perhaps, more likely, it was because Hale knew that only one thing would secure the holiday once and for all. She wrote:

"The Day needs only the sanction of Congress to become established as an American Holiday, not only in the Republic, but wherever Americans meet throughout the world."

In a sense, this was as political as she would get in the magazine. However, Hale would not see any congressional act of the sort that year. Nevertheless, she was likely cheered that the new president, former Union general Ulysses S. Grant, continued the still-new tradition—the third sitting president in a row to do so. In October 1869, President Grant issued his first proclamation for a national day of thanksgiving.

Thomas Nast's thanksgiving illustration for that year was

one of notable inclusion. The Fourteenth Amendment had been ratified in July of the year prior, 1868, which granted citizenship to "[a]ll persons born or naturalized in the United States and subject to the jurisdiction thereof"—which included former enslaved people. It also forbade any state to "make or enforce any law which shall abridge the privileges or immunities of citizen" or "deprive any person of life, liberty, or property, without due process of law," and guaranteed all citizens "equal protection of the laws." The Fourteenth Amendment also had the potential to impact Native peoples. Grant himself was a proponent of citizenship for all, believing that whether one was Protestant or Catholic, Puritan or recently immigrated, all should be able to become an American citizen. His view extended to all Native peoples, whom Grant referred to as the "original occupants of the land" in his inaugural address. He chose his friend Ely Parker as Commissioner of Indian Affairs, making Parker the first Native American ever to hold a cabinet-level post. It also put Parker in a difficult position, as his responsibilities included overseeing policies that ultimately encouraged the assimilation of Indigenous peoples. Grant and Parker wanted citizenship for every Native American, a position with supporters and detractors both in government and among various Indigenous peoples. Grant and Parker's efforts on the citizenship front would be undone by politics, as would their friendship. Parker would eventually resign his post after a political adversary accused him of misappropriating funds (despite Congress clearing him of the fraud charges). Grant's administration would preside over expansionist policies and violence that pushed Native peoples onto reservations, instigating bloody wars and massacres that took lives and compromised the way of life of the nation's "original occupants."

The title for Nast's 1869 illustration was *Uncle Sam's Thanksgiving Dinner.* Uncle Sam presides over a large table populated by different races, genders, and nationalities. "Universal Suffrage" and "Self Governance" form a large centerpiece for the setting and sit squarely in the middle of the table, while "Come One Come All," and "Free and Equal" are splashed across the two lower corners. As Uncle Sam carves a turkey, Columbia occupies the opposite end of the table, sitting with a Black man to her left and engaging with a Chinese man and his family on her right. Diners of varying backgrounds, among them Irish, Italian, German, African American, Native peoples, and more, were a reflection of the changing cultural makeup of the United States. Behind the dinner scene, portraits of Lincoln, Washington, and Grant hang on the wall.

III

A REVOLUTION OF GRACE

For me, every hour is grace. And I feel gratitude in my heart each time I can meet someone and look at his or her smile.

—ELIE WIESEL

CHAPTER 11

MY HEARTFELT PRAYER

There is a difference between a proclamation and an act of Congress and the long march to ratification. Both Lincoln and Hale understood this in different ways. For Lincoln's part, he saw the Thirteenth Amendment passed but did not live to see its final ratification, solidifying it as law.

Hale had witnessed three consecutive presidents help to keep her thanksgiving tradition alive. But she had not yet lived to see it enacted as an official holiday. As it already had in decades prior, thanksgiving would continue to go through many transformations. It would be a reflection of sorts, in the years to come, of the country as it did—and in some cases, did not—evolve.

Grant, in his farewell address to Congress in 1876, said, "It was my fortune, or misfortune, to be called to the office of Chief Executive without any previous political training." His presidency had been plagued by scandal, economic crisis, and corruption, yet it also saw the passage of the Fifteenth Amendment and suffrage for Black men. That same year Grant left office, 1876, Frederick Douglass wrote the editor of the *National Republican* after attending the dedication of the Emancipation Memorial in Washington, DC, an event at which Douglass also spoke and at which Grant, too, was present. "[T]he act by which the negro was made a citizen of the United States and invested with the elective franchise was pre-eminently the act of President U.S. Grant," Douglass wrote, "and this is nowhere seen in the Lincoln monument."

Grant, in his last speech as president, spoke openly of his errors of judgment and mistakes. "I leave comparisons to history," he stated, "claiming only that I have acted in every instance from a conscientious desire to do what was right, constitutional, within the law, and for the very best interests of the whole people. Failures have been errors of judgment, not of intent."

Following in Grant's muddied footsteps came Rutherford B. Hayes. The new president entered office with a good reputation and was considered a man of integrity. Mark Twain predicted great things for the president, who during his term would have to grapple with mounting tensions surrounding Chinese immigration, continued animosity and turmoil with regard to the Native communities and Indian Territories, the ongoing Reconstruction, and a struggle to bolster the nation's depressed economy by returning it to the gold standard.

On what must have appeared a much lighter note, the president also had dealings with Sarah Josepha Hale, who was in her eighty-ninth year when Hayes took office.

Hale had moved to the home of her daughter Frances and Frances's husband, Dr. Lewis Boudinot Hunter, on 1413 Locust Street in Philadelphia, more than a decade earlier. Hale had a large room on the second floor, nearly thirty feet long, where she worked, lived, relaxed, and, of course, read.

The quaint abode had a sleeping alcove, and as it was an upstairs room, its many windows offered sunlight throughout the day. There was a chintz lounge for entertaining, a Franklin stove to keep her warm, a rocking chair for repose and reading, and plenty of room for her collection of books. Hale entertained what appeared to her grandchildren's eyes to be an unending stream of visitors. At other times she kept quiet company with the four pairs of canaries who resided with her, two to a cage, four cages scattered about the room.

There was an amply proportioned desk from which she had continued to edit the *Lady's Book* well into her eighties, as well as to keep up with her legion of correspondents, among them Oliver Wendell Holmes and Charles Dickens.

"Believe me," Dickens wrote Hale from England, "you will never find me departing from those sympathies which we cherish in common and which have won me your esteem and approval." Other correspondents over the years had included writers who were fairly unknown when she had first published them but who had morphed into established literary powerhouses, including Washington Irving, Henry Clay, Nathaniel Hawthorne, and Henry Wadsworth Longfellow. And in addition to these was Hale's final presidential correspondent, Rutherford B. Hayes.

When Hale had written the president, she also sent him

an autographed copy of one of her books. President Hayes, in turn, wrote Hale a personal note of thanks, saying that the book was "prized especially as the gift of a lady who has accomplished so much for the peace and happiness of the American people as yourself."

In his first year in office, Rutherford B. Hayes had become the fourth consecutive president to issue the now familiar annual proclamation, setting aside "Thursday, the 29th of November," 1877, as a day of national thanksgiving. "In all the blessings which depend upon benignant seasons," he wrote, "this has indeed been a memorable year."

And it had been a memorable few years for Hale as well. Unstoppable, in 1874 she had issued yet another edition of *Woman's Record; or, Sketches of All Distinguished Women, from the Creation to A.D. 1868*, notching thirty-six volumes of profiles of women through history—a remarkable feat she had begun with her first volumes in 1853. The front matter included a dedication of sorts: "Inscribed to the Men of America; Who Show, in Their Laws and Customs, Respecting Women, Ideas More Just and Feelings More Noble Than Were Ever Evinced by Men of Any Other Nation: May 'Woman's Record' Meet the Approval of the Sons of Our Great Republic; The World Will Then Know The Daughters are Worthy of Honour." Though vibrant, Hale was less active than in years past. She would often dispatch her grandchildren on errands to the Godey offices in downtown Philadelphia when necessary. Meanwhile, she quite contentedly kept occupied as she sat reading, editing, eating her grapes, and treating her wrinkles, as always, with brown paper and vinegar.

In 1877, Hale sat in her sunny room and wrote what would be her final editorial to the devoted readers of the *Lady's Book*. She reflected not so much on what she had accomplished but focused more on leaving readers with an air of hope and optimism for what the future might hold—for women especially—in years to come.

"And now, having reached my ninetieth year," her swan song editorial began, "I must bid farewell to my countrywomen, with the hope that this work of half a century may be blessed to the furtherance of their happiness and usefulness in their Divinely-appointed sphere. New avenues for higher culture and for good works are opening before them, which fifty years ago were unknown. That they may improve these opportunities, and be faithful to their high vocation, is my heartfelt prayer."

In 1877, Hale's longtime publishing partner and friend, Louis A. Godey, had sold the popular magazine to John Hill Seyes Haulenbeek. After retiring initially to Florida, Godey soon returned to Philadelphia. But his retirement was short-lived. In the year following Hale's farewell article, on November 29, 1878, Louis Godey died unexpectedly. Though he had been ill off and on for several years, and for a time confined to his bed at his home on Chestnut Street, he had recovered. Then, after another sudden onset of illness, he succumbed to what the newspapers described as gout, along with other complications. He was seventy-four years old.

Hale had been born shortly after the founding of the new nation, had witnessed and endured its near destruction, and was now on the other side of the highly contested era of Reconstruction. The woman denied proper schooling in her youth had gone on to become one of the most powerful editors in the country and an advocate for the education of other women like herself. A young widow who had once been faced with raising five children alone was spending the end of her life surrounded by those who loved her. On April 30, 1879, five months after the death of her friend Louis Godey, Sarah Josepha Hale, the "editress," the domestic science maven, the nineteenth-century tastemaker and champion of thanksgiving, died at the age of ninety.

Hale had written her will—"My Last Wishes"—on May 30, 1865, shortly after Abraham Lincoln's death.

The bulk of Hale's will, not surprisingly, described what to do with her vast assortment of books, periodicals, anthologies, and literary ephemera. Aside from those titles already bequeathed to friends and others, the rest were distributed primarily among her surviving children and their respective families. The variation and volume of the collection she was leaving behind was remarkable, a reflection of her life's passion. The works included, in her own shorthand: *Allibone's Dictionary of Authors* (in which Hale's own *Woman's Record* is listed); *The Gallery of American Poetesses*; a collection of poetry penned by English poet Felicia Dorothea Hemans; *The Poems of the Hon. Mrs. Norton*; bound and unbound volumes of the third series of *Littell's Living Age*, a general magazine comprising selections from both English and American publications; *Webster's Dictionary Unabridged*, latest pictorial edition; Ticknor's *History of Spanish Literature*; the voyages of early American Arctic explorer Elisha Kent Kane; John R. Macduff's *The Bow in the Cloud*; and Hale's Bible and prayer book. To her daughters-in-law, in particular, Hale left a copy of *The Female Prose Writers of America*. (Hale, still abhorring the word *female*, was compelled to insert the word *women* in parentheses in the title.) She left them a selection of Scottish poet and playwright Joanna Baillie, John Fleetwood's *Life of Christ*, T. B. Read's *The Female Poets of America* (which Hale of course described as "poetesses" of America), Enoch Arden's *Illustrated Works of the Revolution*, and Hale's mourning book (a Victorian guide to grieving etiquette). There was also a gold card case and a Japanese fan. To her grandchildren went, among others, seven volumes of *Translations from Greek and Roman Literature* and a French dictionary. She was sure to include women writers as well, including *Midsummer Eve: A Fairy Tale of Loving and Being Loved*, by Mrs. S. C. Hall, and *Mrs. Browning's Poems*, a collection of the works of Elizabeth Barrett Browning. She also left her grandchildren a selection of annuals and periodicals, and of course, Hale's own copy of her treasured John Bunyan's *Pilgrim's Progress*. To the smaller grandchildren, she added, "a share in all the little books suitable for them."

Hale left instructions that should the family find any of her finished, unpublished works and manuscripts, they could be forwarded to Francis De Haes Janvier. Janvier was a Philadelphia businessman and fellow poet who was known for writing patriotic works, among them "The Sleeping Sentinel," which he once had the opportunity to read, in a private audience, to President and Mrs. Lincoln. Hale said Janvier would know her wishes regarding her work.

Though most of her works were out of print by the time

of her death, Hale nevertheless remained optimistic about the work she was leaving behind.

"My manuscripts will, I trust, bring a small income annually," she wrote, "this income to be divided equally between my three children. Should it be found best to dispose the copyrights, the money received to be also equally divided."

Finally, in the same document, Hale felt compelled to comment, albeit briefly, on her life's work. "I commenced my Editorial life in January, 1828," she began, "and have steadily pursued it to this day. I leave a large mass of Editorials, Sketches, [manuscripts], and papers; in the care of my son Horatio and wish that he and William would consult with Dr. and Mrs. Hunter and if they find any of these writings worth republishing or any [manuscripts] worth bringing out, I wish them to prepare a series of my works. I have written with an earnest desire to do good."

She had words for her friend Louis Godey as well, who Hale likely assumed would outlive her: "I have no debts save those of love and gratitude to my many kind friends. I wish to thank Mr. Godey, particularly, for his uniform kindness to me during the long time—twenty-seven years—since I have been Editress of the 'Lady's Book': we have never had a difficulty; not a doubt has ever disturbed our friendship."

As for instructions regarding her burial, Hale wrote, "I would be buried in a quiet, private manner in my lot, at the Laurel Hill Cemetery, by the side of my late beloved daughter Josepha."

And so she was. Hale's final resting place was a pine coffin with black cloth, five feet, three and a half inches long, fourteen inches wide, and twelve deep. Ten carriages transported the mourners to a service presided over by Bishop Stevens, the details of which were not advertised to the public. Her coffin's plate read simply:

Sarah Josepha Hale
Born Oct. 24 1788
Died April 30, 1879

Obituaries were widespread, lengthy, and laudatory for both Godey and Hale. Regarding Godey, one biographer said of *Lady's Book*: "Not an immoral thought or profane word can be found in his magazine during the whole five hundred and seventy-one months of its publication."

Hale was repeatedly dubbed the "eminent authoress," a phrase that clearly caught on in the newspapers. "It is but a short time since L. A. Godey, with whom she was so long connected in the editorial work of the *Ladies' Book*, passed over the river, and now she goes to meet him on the other shore."

The *Philadelphia Inquirer* paid tribute to one of its better-known residents, calling Hale a "venerable authoress and editress" whose "pen was always used to elevate and enno-ble, as well as to charm, delight and instruct women, and, by the force of her writings, aided by her own bright example, she did much to dignify women's work. . . . In her death the community loses one who was a bright ornament of it."

Rutherford B. Hayes may have been the last president that Hale ever petitioned. He was not, however, the last president to proclaim the last Thursday of November as a day of national thanksgiving.

Hayes's successor to the presidency, James A. Garfield, was in office for just one hundred twenty days before being shot in the pancreas by a gravely disturbed thirty-nine-year-old lawyer and writer named Charles J. Guiteau. Vice President Chester A. Arthur ascended to the presidency, and continued what Hale predicted would become a tradition.

In Arthur's proclamation of 1881, he wrote, "It has long been the pious custom of our people, with the closing of the year, to look back upon the blessings brought to them in the changing course of the seasons and to return solemn thanks to the allgiving source from whom they flow." The year following, 1882, President Arthur also included a call to citizens to remember those less fortunate. "And I do further recommend," the president wrote, "that the day thus appointed be made a special occasion for deeds of kindness and charity to the suffering and the needy, so that all who dwell within the land may rejoice and be glad in this season of national thanksgiving." The presidential thanksgiving proclamations were also often an opportunity for heads of state to not only call for a unifying day of gratitude but also to draw attention to accomplishments for which to be thankful and, in a way, highlight aspects of policy that the president valued.

That same year saw another proclamation. This one was issued not by a president but rather by the head of another nation, one centuries older than the United States of America.

Roughly fifty years after Andrew Jackson's Indian Removal Act began violently ousting Native peoples from their ancestral homes in the east, forcing more than four thousand to be stockaded, and relocated, to Oklahoma, the head of the Cherokee Nation, Dennis W. Bushyhead, issued a thanksgiving proclamation, one that called for thanks and also drew attention to the ongoing plight of the Indigenous peoples of the United States.

"While thanksgiving days last," Bushyhead wrote, "and are sincerely kept, we need not fear that a magnanimous people will see their government drag and thrust the remnant of our race into the abyss."

Bushyhead issued another thanksgiving proclamation in 1884, again extolling the virtues of thanks and gratitude. He encouraged "renewing the ties of friendship," and charitable acts for the "poor and unfortunate" as well. "In accordance with" President Chester A. Arthur's proclamation, Bushyhead also used the opportunity to address the U.S. government's role in the lives of his people. As shared in the *Council Fire and Arbitrator,* a magazine put out by the National Indian Defense Association, Bushyhead concluded his proclamation that year by prodding his people to pray that "as at this time we gratefully render at the same altar, with our whiter and stronger brothers, our common thanks to God, they may remember that He will deal mercifully and kindly with them as they show magnanimity and justice to their weaker brethren, over whose lives and property they exercise an earthly guardianship."

He affixed the seal of the Cherokee Nation and signed.

In the Cherokee Nation thanksgiving proclamation of

1885, Bushyhead took the opportunity to assert his people's right to land. He wrote that the Cherokee people had "abundant reason to rejoice. They are favored in all things that should make a Nation prosperous and a people happy." Among their blessings were the "indisputable right to an area of land sufficient for the needs of generations of Cherokees to come." Bushyhead's proclamation put forth an optimistic statement of all that he felt was already valued, and might continue to be valued, by and for his people. The Cherokee had, he wrote, a "perfect form of Government, wise laws, unsurpassed educational facilities for their children, and money enough of their own invested to make these blessings permanent." Once again, he mentioned the U.S. government's influence over the lives of his community. "It is true this Nation is neither numerous, wealthy nor powerful compared with many others," he wrote, "but it stands and relies upon the plighted faith of a Nation that has become the strongest on earth by reason of its respect for human rights." He reminded his fellow citizens: "While the Cherokees have cause to be deeply grateful, let us not forget that acknowledgment of blessings implies a sense of responsibility for their proper use. With these thoughts, let us continue the Christian custom of National Thanksgiving, practiced by the Cherokees since they became a Christian people."

He signed the proclamation "in acknowledgment and gratitude to the Great Spirit for his many favors and dispensations."

In 1891, Bushyhead's successor, Principal Chief Joel B.

Mayes, issued his own proclamation joining with President Benjamin Harrison, "our great father, the President of the United States." The year before, in 1890, Harrison had issued a proclamation making it illegal for the Cherokee to issue leases or grazing contracts on what was called the Cherokee Outlet: more than eight million acres of land held by the Cherokee Nation. These leases had been the source of much-needed income. Mayes wrote that he hoped the Cherokee People "may continue in the peaceful possession of their land and homes to a time without end," and appointed Thursday, November 26, 1891, "a day of Thanksgiving and Praise to God, that He still permits the Cherokee Nation of Indians to live in the enjoyment of this civil and religious liberty, and in this struggle for the right of soil and self-government, ask Him to shield us from all danger."

In December, the Cherokee were forced to sell nearly seven million acres of land for roughly $1.27 per acre—a fraction of what the acreage was worth to land-hungry settlers on the open market. By spring of 1893, Congress authorized the purchase. That fall, one hundred thousand settlers lined up their wagons, and at the firing of a pistol, rushed in to claim parcels of that land for themselves. The so-called Cherokee Strip Land Run became the largest in Oklahoma history.

CHAPTER 12

POMP AND CHANGING CIRCUMSTANCE

In 1876, just three years before Hale's death, the first Thanksgiving Day football game was played between Yale and Princeton, for the American Intercollegiate Football Association championship—though the game still evidenced its rugby roots. In the years to come, those two teams soon became Thanksgiving Day regulars, and it was not long before numerous high school and college football teams began to hold games on the holiday. It may not have been what Hale envisioned, but traditions evolve, often in unexpected ways and for unpredictable reasons.

In Sarah Josepha Hale's own lifetime, the celebration and tradition of thanksgiving had morphed between and conflated cultural, ancient, religious, and secular customs. Establishing a national day—not a date—associated with giving thanks allowed for increased coalescing around what was becoming a newly fixed, yet increasingly malleable tradition. In addition to her campaigning for the holiday itself, Hale's endless hostessing tips and descriptions for how one might best celebrate—whether discussing the overladen table in her novel *Northwood*, or sharing her white wine vinegar dressing for fish or "soodjee" with the readers of the *Lady's Book*—further codified the event.

Some concepts surrounding a thanksgiving commemoration eventually became somewhat less frequent however, including the issuance of presidential proclamations for days of thanksgiving *other* than the one that now fell at the end of November. The custom of proclaiming days of fasting and prayer, or thanksgivings for various military achievements, slowly ebbed and fell away without much notice, like the last few scraps off a turkey's carcass. President Benjamin Harrison, in April 1889, issued a proclamation of thanksgiving to honor the centennial of George Washington's inauguration. The thanksgiving proclamations that remained, year after year, were those pertaining to the holiday Hale had envisioned.

In the 1890s, the media took note of the cultural landscape of the day, some noting that in years past the holiday might have been given scant notice, whereas it was now a main fixture on the calendar. The celebration of the holiday also became a reflection of the nation's changing population. The turn of the century saw a drastic increase in immigrant communities throughout the country, especially in major metropolitan areas.

In honor of Thanksgiving Day in 1897, the *Chicago Tribune* highlighted varying celebrations among the different ethnic groups within their city. "Alien Residents of Chicago Feel Spirit of Thanks" was the title of just one article on a two-page spread in the newspaper. "Foreign born citizens of America will see to it that the observance of Thanksgiving . . . does not pass away. . . . Investigation shows that if the old-time 'rejoicing after the harvest' is losing any of the essence of praise and gratitude, it is losing it among the very people who express the fear that it may be lost. As the American loosens his grip upon this feast of his fathers, the foreigner tightens his grasp and last hold on that which he considered good." The newspaper shared stories from a local fisherman—"Peg" Ecks—who caught his dinner in Lake Michigan and "dined in solitude on the Lake Shore within the shadow of millionaires' homes." Editors also visited the Polish, Italian, Swedish, German, French, and "Bohemian" communities, describing how each chose to celebrate in their adopted home. "There are three kinds of Bohemians in Chicago . . . ," the editors wrote, "the Hussites, the Catholics, and the Free Thinkers, but one and all will celebrate this semi-religious and purely American festival of Thanksgiving."

The publication further captured the evolution of the day, writing, "I have noticed the growth of the Thanksgiving spirit, in a holiday sense, among the Bohemians and among other people of foreign birth. It may seem passing strange one day if the life of the festival depends upon those to whom its spirit was at one time thought foreign."

Not to be left out, the non–meat eaters of the city celebrated as well, and the menu at the Vegetarian club of the University of Chicago included mock turtle soup with quenelles, chartreuse of cranberries, and potatoes en pyramid with mushrooms.

Of course, one of the key tenets of Hale's holiday, as well as thanksgivings and harvest festivals since time immemorial, remained intact: the concept of gratitude. And by the turn of the twentieth century, charity, too, became even more closely associated with the thanksgiving holiday and was encouraged as a means of celebrating the day.

"While we all give thanks, truly and from grateful hearts, 'let us scatter beams of sunshine,'" wrote the editors of the *New Education* in their November 1898 edition. The stated aim of the monthly publication out of New York City was "inspiration," its motto "Not what we promise—but what we do." Subscriptions were one dollar a year and advertising rates three dollars per column inch. The publication featured book reviews and language lessons, readings in geography and advice on writing, poetry, and history. With regard to Thanksgiving Day, the opening editorial reminded readers to remember those who had gone to the "land of perpetual thanksgiving" since the previous year. "Can we not put aside our pleasures for an hour or two, and 'weep with those who weep' at this, their first lonely Thanksgiving Day? . . . And let us all try to see the bright side more, the dull one less, and to emphasize the blessings instead of always mentioning the afflictions which must drop into every life, and which we must not, therefore, expect to escape. But even these have a bright side, if only we will learn to look for it. . . . Let us be thankful . . . to develop the 'bettermost' side of ourselves, and at the same time not forget those who need our help. . . . And finally, let us be doubly grateful for the troubles that we have escaped!"

Hale and her role in the custom were not mentioned in that lengthy editorial, nor in the extensive spread in the *Tribune*. But as the twentieth century dawned, distance increased from Lincoln's proclamation, the tradition seemed firmly fixed on the November calendar, and the media began to look *back* at what they thought were the origins of the holiday. Lincoln was most often credited, but Sarah Josepha Hale's name was eventually included in these backward glances.

A two-page spread in a November 1916 issue of the *Journal and Tribune* out of Knoxville, Tennessee, announced: "Thanksgiving Proclamations of Our Presidents: The Evolution of Thanksgiving Documents from George Washington's Quill Pen Proclamation to President Wilson's Call to Thanksgiving Written by Himself on a Typewriter." The newspaper offered a survey of sorts of the holiday over the years, stating, "Our Thanksgiving Day belongs to all the people of our land, of whatever creed or race." The article asserted that the holiday's roots reached back to Holland in 1575, where the "English pilgrims" lived before traveling to what would become Massachusetts. The piece also devoted a significant section to Hale and asserted there was much to be thankful for in 1916, as the United States had avoided the "ravages of war." In five months, that would all change.

President Woodrow Wilson's 1916 Thanksgiving Day proclamation referenced the conflict already tearing Europe apart. "In the midst of our peace and happiness," Wilson wrote, "our thoughts dwell with painful disquiet upon the struggles and sufferings of the nations at war and of the peoples upon whom war has brought disaster without choice or possibility of escape on their part. We cannot think of our own happiness without thinking also of their pitiful distress."

By the following April, the United States declared war on Germany.

No one had seen anything like the Great War in their lifetime, and all corners of the nation felt its effects. Thanksgiving itself, during wartime, was tweaked by many to reflect the current struggle. The United States Food Administration—headed by Herbert Hoover—had already established a number of food-saving efforts, including "meatless Monday" and "wheatless Wednesday" (both of which maintain popularity in America today). USFA posters and propaganda insisted "Food will win the war," and implored families to sign petitions stating they would adhere to the restrictions. As the holiday approached, the agency and the media urged citizens to "Hooverize" their thanksgivings, in order to better reserve supplies and food stores for troops and allies overseas. Businesses and hotels complied as well. One newspaper in Santa Barbara, California, offered menus that could be tailored to these patriotic suggestions. The menus were "guaranteed," the paper promised, "to do justice to the occasion and at the same time conserve the food most needed for the successful prosecution of the war."

Similar advice was found in publications across the country, and the suggestions were variations on common culinary themes: No granulated sugar in the cranberry sauce or in pies—use brown sugar or molasses instead. No meat "in the making of your soup."

So when the holiday in that war-torn year came around, the press suggested stuffing the turkey with oysters or chestnuts to save bread. Making plum pudding egg-free. Ice cream was suggested for dessert, and though it fell on what one newspaper described as "ice-creamless Thursday," it was assumed that an exception would be made for the holiday.

In his proclamation of 1917, President Wilson wrote that stopping to give thanks was a "custom we can follow now even in the midst of the tragedy of a world shaken by war and immeasurable disaster, in the midst of sorrow and great peril, because even amidst the darkness that has gathered about us we can see the great blessings God has bestowed upon us, blessings that are better than mere peace of mind and prosperity of enterprise."

One year hence, in November 1918, the war was over. Germany and the allies signed their armistice agreement on November 11.

One reader wrote to the *New York Times* on Armistice Day, likening the day's rejoicing to a thanksgiving, calling it the "most spontaneous, and, on the whole, the most generous in spirit of any within the memory of the present generation." The letter continued, "Should not the spirit of this day be perpetuated? Would not humanity be the better for a universal holiday consecrated to international ideals, to brotherly love among peoples? . . . Is there not a place at this season of the year for a holiday devoted to the feeling of thanksgiving and of human brotherhood, and can these feelings be associated with any event better than with that to to-day, when peace, we hope permanent, has been given to the world?"

Wilson's proclamation for Thanksgiving Day 1918 was issued on November 16, just five days after the signing of the armistice.

"It has long been our custom to turn in the autumn of the year in praise and thanksgiving," the president began. "This year we have special and moving cause to be grateful and to rejoice. God has in His good pleasure given us peace."

It was a lot to be thankful for, in America and far beyond her shores, but despite the coming cessation of hostilities, the world did not enjoy freedom from concern that year. There was yet another foe to be bested, one that had been ravaging citizens across the globe since January.

Eventually killing more than fifty million people throughout the world—quite possibly more—the influenza pandemic took the lives of 675,000 individuals in the United States alone. The so-called Spanish flu was an H1N1 virus that devastated the planet, snuffing out people from all walks of life, even the young and healthy. Its grasp reached all corners the earth, even the Arctic, and the number of infections was estimated to be one-third of the world's population—nearly five hundred million. The war had played a role in its spread as well, as did a reluctance to act early on in the epidemic. When censors decided to downplay the severity of the deadly illness in order to keep morale up during the war, the resulting failure to act more decisively and critically would prove deadly for millions.

Then the flu mutated, shifting in order to survive, and created an even more deadly second wave, which hit the

United States and other countries still months before the war's end. The deadliest month of the Spanish flu was October 1918. November's thanksgiving would necessarily be very different—especially since the most effective way of preventing infections was isolation, quarantine, and a limit on public gatherings.

The joy and relief of the end of the Great War was overshadowed by this invisible, deadly enemy. There was a desire for unity, coming together with loved ones who had been in harm's way, or uniting around the memory of those who would be at the table no more. But that quite human desire had to be quelled.

In a typical missive of the day, the November 28 issue of the *Deseret Evening News* in Salt Lake City, Utah, noted that the day was "impressively observed," that "gratitude" for the war's end was a staple sentiment of the occasion, and those less fortunate were remembered. However, there were "no public functions." "The day is being observed also as a day for helping the needy and spreading good cheer," the paper said, noting: "Quarantine interferes. Owing to the influenza quarantine, the day's festivities . . . had to be postponed till Christmas day. But Thanksgiving services of some sort are being held in nearly every home. . . . Many others, including state and city officials, have expressed the opinion that this should be the most important thanksgiving day in the history of the country." There would be food at the hospitals, infirmaries and jails, but "Because the influenza quarantine prevents public gatherings, the day in Utah is being observed quietly and without any spectacular features."

Some state entities, such as the state board of health in

Nebraska, warned citizens to be specifically aware of the potential for a flu flare-up during the holiday weekend. The desire to join together overrode common sense for some. In Ohio, for example, festivities proved calamitous. The *Ohio State Journal* reported that twenty-seven new cases of influenza could be traced to a single family meal on Thanksgiving Day:

"27 Ill as a Result of Holiday Party"—Family Dinner on Thanksgiving Spread the Flu, Dr. Kahn Says

The horror of the epidemic swept into the Christmas season as well. A week after thanksgiving, the *St. Paul Daily News* in Minnesota announced, "Santa Claus is Down with the Flu—Appearances in Minneapolis Stores Banned—10 More St. Paul Deaths."

There were those who looked to the spirit of thanksgiving despite the circumstances. In Davenport, Iowa, the newspaper proclaimed "an excellent cause for thankfulness," as the town reported only 83 cases of flu on Thanksgiving Day—down from 147 the day before.

Many soldiers were still abroad in late November. "A Solemn Day Overseas," the *Kansas City Star* reported. "Yanks Observe the Nation's Most Heartfelt Thanksgiving." The article described troops camped along the Moselle and Sauer rivers, awaiting their time to march into Prussia and having their own celebration, with a feast of extra rations and an afternoon of games in camp. Though turkey was not necessarily on the menu, the "Salvation Army lassies and Red

Cross girls" baked pies and made doughnuts for the soldiers. The local villages quartering American troops decorated their homes with evergreens. The newspaper noted that two and a half million Americans were in Europe observing the "most solemn and heartfelt Thanksgiving since the birth of the Nation."

But some in the states were ready for a particular thanksgiving tradition to end—one neither Hale nor anyone before her had anticipated.

"On Thanksgiving Day, in a walk of six blocks, I was accosted by thirty boys and girls in grotesque costume," a reader wrote to the editor of the *New York Times*, "each of whom demanded money for Thanksgiving. . . . Is there no way in which the thing can be put a stop to?" The letter was signed, "An American."

The strange tradition of "thanksgiving masking" had been going on for decades, and by the end of the century it was customary for children and adults in costume to hit the streets dressed as political and historic figures. Shops did a brisk business in the sale of masks as well as candies, which they began to display alongside one another during the season. There were horned adults and confetti-strewn streets, with popular costumes including the "ragamuffin." Kids dressed in tattered clothing wandered the streets asking strangers for money or treats. This particular outfit and practice became so popular in New York that the city had a nickname for the holiday: "Ragamuffin Day." On occasion, the streets of the metropolis even hosted ragamuffin parades.

As the twentieth century progressed, this strange tradition died away, eventually replaced by another treat-seeking, masking tradition: Halloween. And the tradition of parades would be elevated to new prominence, as thanksgiving's personality morphed yet again.

In August 1920, the Wilson administration and the nation saw the ratification of the Nineteenth Amendment, giving women the right to vote. Though Hale had not lobbied actively for that right during her lifetime, it seems a development that she may have applauded and likely would have written about in the pages of the *Lady's Book*. Prohibition had gone into effect in January, perhaps limiting the tenor of celebration of that or any other subsequent event.

The American Professional Football Association (later the NFL) was also born that year. On Thanksgiving Day, the Akron Pros defeated the Canton Bulldogs 7–0, and it helped earn them the championship title—which at the time was based on win record rather than on a specific game. As champions, the Akron players earned a football-shaped gold fob. In the coming years, the sport would continue to be associated with the holiday in grand form. It was a needed bright spot in a somewhat dismal year for sports. Just a month earlier, in October 1920, other sporting news was darker, with the Chicago White Sox being dubbed the "Black Sox" in the papers for throwing the 1919 World Series.

Election Day, November 2, 1920, heralded a landslide victory for Warren G. Harding and his veep, Calvin "Silent Cal" Coolidge. The country appeared to be moving in a more peaceful direction. Coming off the flu and the war, Americans craved joy and diversion—and maybe a drink. The former was easily obtained. The latter, well, not for some time yet.

With a bit of distance from the war and the spirit of the Roaring Twenties starting to rear its illicit, gin-soaked head, the holiday season was set to be a promising one—especially for shopkeepers and businesses. Over the years, thanksgiving activities had become more closely associated with Christmas shopping. Advertising for that December fete had become increasingly common in November. Gimbel Brothers Department Store in Philadelphia was no different; their advertising kicked into high gear come November.

"Gimbel Toy Store leads the town!" one such ad proclaimed. "Let no child miss it.—Gimbels, Philadelphia, Fourth floor." Gimbel Brothers advertised "pre-war prices or lower" for their lace lingerie. Crepe de chine bloomers were $1.85 and $2.95. "And the cutest 'Creepers'" (a blousier version of a romper for babies and toddlers) at "$2.95 and $3.95." On the same ad-packed page came a suggestion to "give pleasure to a lot of children who can't do a thing for you in return. Bring them—in the mornings—to the Gimbel Toy Store. Have them ride on real ponies."

But ten days later, Gimbel Brothers Department Store changed the holiday game forever when fifty of their employees, many dressed as elves, marched from the Philadelphia Museum of Art to Eighth and Market Streets. Ellis Gimbel, in a clever marketing move, had the affair culminate inside the store's "Toyland." Upon reaching Gimbels, the parade's featured reveler, Santa—looking perhaps more like a thief in the night than a jolly old soul—scaled five stories of the department store's exterior with the help of the fire department and entered not through a chimney, but through a window, and into the store. There he waited to welcome shoppers. It was not, however, the nation's first holiday parade. That distinction went to the Santa Claus Parade of Peoria, Illinois, first held in 1887 and continuing to this day. But thanksgiving parades were about to become an even greater a spectacle.

In 1924, four years after Gimbel Brothers held their 1920 procession through the streets of Philadelphia, the R. H. Macy & Company store in New York City upped the ante. In what must have seemed an audacious move, the department store unveiled what was then called the Macy's Christmas Parade. There were bands and horse-drawn floats, shrewdly designed to match Macy's Christmas window displays. That year, the windows were adorned with scenes from the Mother Goose rhymes, including "There Was an Old Woman Who Lived in a Shoe." Employees in costume marched in the parade as well. Animals borrowed from the Central Park Zoo appeared, too—among them elephants, camels, and bears. The passenger on the very last float was Santa Claus. Not to be outdone, Gimbels stepped up its game in 1925, adding many more floats and lengthening its route, which it posted in full in at least one Philadelphia newspaper.

These marvelous new spectacles were not without incident. In 1930, the Gimbels Santa float got stuck in trolley tracks that lined the streets of Philadelphia—and Santa got tossed from his "sleigh" and ended up at Hahnemann Hospital. Old Nick pulled through and made it back in time to climb through the window and help Gimbels sell toys.

Despite new parades and pomp surrounding this growing holiday tradition, thanksgiving still existed at the behest of the commander in chief, as well as state governors, who annually decided whether they would follow suit with the day the president had chosen. In fact, few Americans ever paid attention to the annual proclamations, as that late November Thursday had become an entrenched custom.

That is, until 1939.

The 1939 thanksgiving proclamation would turn out to be unique for several reasons. At the time there were far more immediate concerns for the country, and the future of the holiday was hardly foremost in people's minds, if only because its occurrence had long been taken for granted. Yet the tradition passionately campaigned for by Hale and maintained annually by presidents from Lincoln on was, in fact, nearly upended on Roosevelt's watch—and it was also during his tenure that thanksgiving achieved a major milestone, one Hale had long desired but never lived to see.

CHAPTER 13

MILESTONES AND MISSTEPS

The first proclamations from the desk of President Franklin D. Roosevelt regarding thanksgiving came and went with the usual notice—which, by the 1930s, was not much. It had become almost a foregone conclusion that come October or November, the president would issue a proclamation for the last Thursday in November—as expected. Shortly after, individual states' governors would issue their own thanksgiving proclamations for their respective states, citing the same day the president had chosen—also as expected.

Technology had increased the White House's ability to communicate more regularly and more directly with the American public, and President Roosevelt made good use of these developments. Warren G. Harding had installed the first radio in the White House. His successor, Calvin Coolidge, became the first president to ever broadcast live from the commander in chief's residence. Beginning in 1933, Franklin D. Roosevelt took presidential radio addresses to an entirely new level with his "Fireside Chats."

Roosevelt used the chats to speak "directly" to Americans who were gathered around their own radios throughout the nation. Chats sometimes focused on specific topics, such as banking, the Recovery Act or congressional developments, the Works Progress Administration, or the Farm Security Administration. The tone and tenor of the talks were often designed to be reassuring as much as informative.

On November 24, 1938, Thanksgiving Day, Roosevelt broadcasted from what was known as the "Little White House"—his southern retreat in Warm Springs, Georgia. He relaxed in a quaint cottage in the pines while there, often with family and friends. After contracting polio in 1921, the president found swimming in the area's mineral pools to be rejuvenating and soothing. Roosevelt's thanksgiving proclamation that year mentioned George Washington and Abraham Lincoln, stating that the observance of the holiday "was consecrated when George Washington issued a Thanksgiving proclamation in the first year of his presidency." He finished by acknowledging growing trouble in Europe. "In the time of our fortune," Roosevelt wrote, "it is fitting that we offer prayers for unfortunate people in other lands who are in dire distress at this our Thanksgiving Season."

Live from Warm Springs, Roosevelt brought Americans into his family's thanksgiving celebration, sharing their joy and activities. He also spoke of new developments at Warm Springs itself, including the recent establishment of the National Foundation for Infantile Paralysis. "This Thanksgiving

Day we have much to be thankful for," Roosevelt said during his chat, sharing that he had received many telegrams on the occasion, including one from actor and comedian Eddie Cantor, who wrote, "I am thankful that I can live in a country where our leaders sit down on Thanksgiving Day to carve up a turkey instead of a Nation."

Technology continued its march forward and was on grand display that spring during the 1939 New York World's Fair in Flushing Meadows, Queens, which opened on April 30. "The World of Tomorrow" was the slogan of the fair, which focused solidly on the future. Albert Einstein attended, presenting a speech on cosmic rays. The monolithic Trylon—more than six hundred feet tall—towered over an eighteen-story globe known as the Perisphere, which offered visitors the chance to view a model of a future city called "Democracity." A seven-foot-tall robot named Elektro prowled the fairgrounds as well. Dupont debuted the first-ever nylon pantyhose, a welcome, sturdy replacement to wool and silk. The firms Westinghouse, General Electric, Crosley, and RCA, ever at one another's throats, each debuted a fascinating new appliance called the television. President Roosevelt attended the fair as well, and his speech to the nation was broadcast over RCA's fledgling station, W2XBS—which later became WNBC—making him the first president to appear on television. At the time, there were an estimated one hundred to two hundred televisions tuned in, netting Roosevelt a probable audience of a whopping one thousand.

Later that year, the news grew darker. In September, Germany invaded Poland. Declarations of war followed, thrusting Europe into World War II. That fall Roosevelt made news for an unexpected reason, and thanksgiving became slightly more controversial.

The complaints had been stacking up for a good chunk of Roosevelt's presidency. As the holiday of thanksgiving had continued to evolve, so had its association with the Christmas shopping season. That link had grown even stronger as the recently established parades in Philadelphia and New York literally welcomed Santa Claus to the season and physically led shoppers to department stores on St. Nick's heels.

In 1939, the *expected* Thanksgiving—the last Thursday of November—was to fall on November 30, just as it had in 1933, during Roosevelt's first year in office. That year, the National Retail Dry Goods Association had lobbied the president hard, urging him to proclaim thanksgiving seven days earlier, on November 23. Other merchants and manufacturers joined the movement. John G. Bullock, of Bullock's department stores in Los Angeles, wrote to Senator William McAdoo, making perhaps the self-interested claim that moving up the date would impact "distribution activities across the entire United States," and the potential to "increase employment and purchasing power." Other retailers also pled with the president to move up the date. However, in 1933, Roosevelt refused. The *New York Times* reported that, among other issues, such a change would "disarrange football games which are scheduled for Thanksgiving."

Now, six years later, the National Retail Dry Goods Association reemerged with their rallying cry. In an attempt to pacify merchants and retailers, the White House tossed out numerous ideas. At one point during the back-and-forth, Roosevelt even suggested moving the holiday to a Monday in the middle of November. He consulted with politicians, clergy, and other experts, among them Columbia University professor James T. Shotwell from the Carnegie Endowment for International Peace. Shotwell did not share the concerns of the retailers, but rather hoped the country might "recapture the spirit [of Thanksgiving] through which the emphasis would be placed on spiritual rather than material things."

Retailer lobbying started early in 1939 and showed little sign of abating. That summer, Roosevelt announced at a press conference that rather than the last Thursday of November— November 30—he would instead declare the previous Thursday, the twenty-third, to be the national day of thanks. When making the announcement, Roosevelt observed that Thanksgiving Day "seems to be the only holiday that is not provided by law, nationally." To support this decision, he offered that the holiday, prior to the Civil War, had been a "moveable feast . . . so there is nothing sacred about it."

This, of course, had been Hale's nightmare. She had long predicted—and feared—that without an act of Congress, mere convenience would upend her hard-won tradition. She did not intend her favored feast to be a movable one.

The press erupted at Roosevelt's news, and while retailers rejoiced, numerous sectors of society panicked. School vacations would be affected. Football coaches were up in arms about the disruption of long-held traditional battles. New York University's Board of Athletic Control wrote with concern about the school's annual football bout with Fordham

held in Yankee Stadium on Thanksgiving Day. Calendar printers, especially, were apoplectic. "I am afraid your change for
Thanksgiving is going to cause the calendar manufacturers
untold grief," wrote John Taylor of the Budget Press in Sa-
lem, Ohio.

And while some larger businesses claimed they would
benefit from the move, other entrepreneurs felt differently.
"The small storekeeper would prefer leaving Thanksgiving
Day where it belongs," wrote Charles Arnold, of Arnold's
Men's Shop Inc. "If the large department stores are over-
crowded during the shorter shopping period before Christmas, the overflow will come, naturally, to the neighborhood
store." Owners of smaller shops had been waiting years for
a late thanksgiving to give them a boost, he continued, writing, "we are sadly disappointed at your action."

Some citizens took a lighter approach:

> *Mr. President:*
>
> *I see by the paper this morning where you want
> to change Thanksgiving Day to November 23 of
> which I heartily approve. Thanks.*
>
> *Now, there are some things that I would like
> done and would appreciate your approval:*
>
> *1. Have Sunday changed to Wednesday;*
> *2. Have Monday's to be Christmas;*
> *3. Have it strictly against the Will of God to
> work on Tuesday;*
> *4. Have Thursday to be Pay Day with time
> and one-half for overtime;*

5. *Require everyone to take Friday and
   Saturday off for a fishing trip down the
   Potomac.*

*With these in view and hoping you will give
me some consideration at your next Congress, I
remain,*

> *Yours very truly*
> *Shelby O. Bennett*

Now it fell to the governors of the individual states to support Roosevelt's new date . . . or not.

President Roosevelt stuck to his guns, going so far as to designate November 21 of the *following* year, 1940—the *third* Thursday of the month, rather than the last—as Thanksgiving Day. This was most likely done to pacify the calendar industry, giving them a head start on their publishing schedule.

Though the 1939 date had already been announced to the press that summer, Roosevelt publicly issued what had already become a rather contentious proclamation on Halloween of that year, saying, as always, how much there was to be thankful for: "As a Nation we are deeply grateful that in a world of turmoil we are at peace with all countries, and we especially rejoice in the strengthened bonds of our friendship with the other peoples of the Western Hemisphere."

He again paid tribute to George Washington's 1789 proclamation, but this time omitted Abraham Lincoln. "It is fitting," Roosevelt wrote, "that we should continue this hallowed custom and select a day in 1939 to be dedicated to reverent thoughts of thanksgiving."

For the first time in anyone's memory, half the state governors defied the president and issued proclamations for the "original," anticipated date—the thirtieth. Mississippi, Texas, and Colorado observed *both* the twenty-third and the thirtieth. A Bryan, Texas, newspaper wrote on November 30, "Americans have reason enough to make use of two Thanksgiving days." In an article titled "Thanksgiving Day Mixup Has Extended Right into Roosevelt's Own Family," the *Fort Worth Star-Telegram* listed the different days that various members of Roosevelt's own extended family would be celebrating. The choices were largely dependent on where those Roosevelts were located and what their own traditions were. Either way, either day, Americans celebrated the holiday(s) in the usual fashion. No matter the date, they were grateful the country was not at war.

President Roosevelt's 1939 Thanksgiving Day Proclamation was significant in another way as well, one that few would have noticed at the time, as so much emphasis was placed on the fact that the president had upended the expected date. Even today, the most striking thing about this proclamation would go unnoticed by modern readers. President Roosevelt was the first president, ever, to mention Pilgrims in his proclamation.

For 1939, illustrator J. C. Leyendecker had painted a simple concept for the cover of the *Saturday Evening Post*: a turkey sitting in a tree. The fowl looks almost as if it is deciding where to land—on the twenty-third or the thirtieth. Meanwhile, in the background, a small boy and his dog look on as Grandpa sharpens his ax. The magazine published its issue on a convenient Saturday falling between the two holidays—November 25.

Where the mid- to late nineteenth century had Thomas Nast and *Harper's Weekly*, so the mid-twentieth century had Leyendecker, his younger admirer Norman Rockwell, and the *Saturday Evening Post*. It was arguably the most powerful magazine in the country, appearing like clockwork each week in nearly three million American homes—and circulation continued to grow. The magazine's art and illustrations were often a reflection—as Thomas Nast's illustrations were in his times—of the mood of the country, or at least the mood as perceived by the artist and the publication's editors.

Over the years, Leyendecker's annual holiday covers varied from nostalgic to sardonic. In 1907, a Pilgrim is depicted stalking an unsuspecting turkey. In 1920, however, an alarmed Pilgrim recoils as arrows whiz by his ear, piercing the roasted bird on the table in front of him. Title: *Startled Pilgrim*. In December 1923, a rare post–Thanksgiving Day cover image was dubbed *Trading for a Turkey*, and portrayed the Pilgrim in question as more of a shady salesman than the founder of any respectable feast.

In November 1928, a buff, strapping Pilgrim with a blunderbuss tossed over his shoulder stood defiantly staring down his rival . . . a college footballer. The 1928 cover highlighted two aspects of the holiday that had begun to take hold in American culture in the early twentieth century—football and Pilgrims. The artist depicting this Pilgrim-leatherhead face-off was again Leyendecker. However, the legend at the bottom of this cover read "Thanksgiving: 1628–1928"—not the 1621 date modern-day Americans might habitually peg as the "first" occurrence of thanksgiving.

The conflation of thanksgivings, days of fasting and humiliation, harvest festivals, and more had long predated Hale's campaigns. The feasting associated with the holiday had taken root in New England, and was no doubt influenced by the region's Puritan roots and that population's early desire to distance themselves from Christmas celebrations, which were considered indulgent, pagan, and possibly heretical.

While Puritans wanted to reform the Anglican Church, Pilgrims wanted a clean break from the scene altogether. Pilgrims had left England for Holland before coming to North America, eventually returning briefly to England in order to sail across the Atlantic, landing in what would become New England in 1620. Their first year in their new home did not go well; the Pilgrims found it harder to survive than they had anticipated. In April 1621, Pilgrims formed a treaty with the nearby Wampanoag. Their leader, Ousamequin—often referred to by his title, Massasoit—had offered these newcomers his protection and more than a little instruction about how to survive in the climate and successfully tend the land. The Wampanoag had their own conflicts in the region to worry about, and prior interactions between them and European explorers—going back to the 1500s and increasing drastically in the early 1600s—often resulted in sickness and wanton violence. The land that the Pilgrims occupied had been the site of a village of Indigenous peoples that had been eradicated by disease. The devastated Wampanoag were wary but also in need of allies and weapons, hence the treaty that was struck in early 1621. At some point in the fall of 1621, after a successful harvest, the Pilgrims ate better than they had in some time.

That November, in a cover letter accompanying a report to their financial backers in England, Edward Winslow, assistant to the governor of Plymouth Colony, William Bradford, wrote the following:

> *Our harvest being gotten in, our governor sent four men on fowling, that so we might after a more special manner rejoice together after we had gathered the fruit of our labors; they four in one day killed as much fowl as, with a little help beside, served the Company almost a week, at which time, amongst other Recreations, we exercised our Arms, many of the Indians coming amongst us, and among the rest their greatest king Massasoit, with some ninety men, whom for three days we entertained and feasted, and they went out and killed five Deer, which they brought to the Plantation and bestowed on our Governor, and upon the Captain and others.*

These lines above are literally all that is known of the 1621 gathering with the Wampanoag. When Governor Bradford himself later wrote a history of his time in Plymouth, titled *Of Plimouth Plantation*, he did not mention a gathering with the Wampanoag, but rather focused on the welcome abundance of food. It seems the Pilgrims themselves did not place much significance on that 1621 event.

Sometime later, in November 1621, the ironically named ship *Fortune* brought more colonists to the Pilgrim settlement, but no supplies. More Pilgrim arrivals meant less food. Tensions between the Pilgrims and the Native peoples increased. Bloodshed ensued. The Great Puritan Migration continued, as what eventually became New England grew and expanded. Ousamequin died in 1660, and almost from the moment of his death onward, relations between his sons, their people, and the European newcomers became increasingly fraught as the English began to far outnumber, and exploit, the Indigenous people. Fifteen years after Ousamequin's death, King Philip's War erupted. Ousamequin's son Metacom—in English, "Philip"—led a confederation of Native peoples into battle against the newcomers. At least three thousand Native Americans were killed. Many others were sold into slavery. After returning home, Metacom was betrayed, killed, beheaded, and quartered. His head was displayed on a pike in Plymouth for twenty-five years.

The interesting thing about the thanksgiving story Americans grew up hearing is that in all of Sarah Josepha Hale's letters to the presidents—including the one sent to Lincoln— not once did she mention the Pilgrims or 1621 or Ousamequin. And not once did Lincoln, in his proclamations, replete with sincere intentions and humble prose, with their calls for gratitude, make a single reference to the Pilgrims or the

Puritans or the 1621 event or any events occurring in Plymouth. The proclamation that Seward penned and which Lincoln signed said nothing whatsoever about feasts with neighboring Native peoples or the *Mayflower* or the Wampanoag. Lincoln's documents mentioned nothing of what the Pilgrims ate on this day; it recalled nothing of that harsh winter. If anything, his documents were, rather, a harkening back to thanksgivings—those with a little *t*—of old. Those that looked to bounties in the midst of scarcity, those that found grace in the midst of strife, those that acknowledged loss yet embraced what few and fleeting gains there appeared to be.

In the years immediately following Lincoln, when the press spoke of thanksgiving, it was often to vaguely mention early New England Puritan traditions and Pilgrim forefathers. Soon, though, interpretations and embellishments of the story of these early American settlers began to work their way into newspapers and magazines, and therefore into homes and culture. This romanticization coincided with growing anti-immigrant sentiment in the later nineteenth century and an aggrandizement of Anglo-Saxon heritage.

One of the first, widely read works on the story of thanksgiving was an 1869 article in the popular *Our Young Folks: An Illustrated Magazine for Boys and Girls*, written by J. H. A. Bone. Titled "The First New England Thanksgiving," this work seems to be at least partially responsible for the embracing of the novelization of the history, and would sound familiar to any child growing up in America in the latter half of the twentieth century, when images from 1973's *A Charlie Brown Thanksgiving* and 1988's "The *Mayflower* Voyagers" embedded themselves in the cultural consciousness. Though intended for young readers, Bone's article was reprinted in newspapers across the country that year. Nearly twenty years later, in 1887, *Demorest's Monthly Magazine* reprinted Bone's entire story again—but this time credited the tale to H. Maria George. It is clear from a survey of nineteenth-century journalism and books that thanksgiving's history has always been challenging for the media.

In 1875, the *New York Times* reflected on what it considered to be the hundred-year anniversary of Thanksgiving, citing the 1775 proclamation issued during the Revolutionary War. In 1890, in an article titled "A National Thanksgiving. The Custom Not Really Established Until 1862. It Is a New-England Holiday, But the Turkey Comes from the South," it reviewed some previous presidentially proclaimed thanksgivings, the fleeting nature of the day itself, and then glossed over its murkier history. "There has been some controversy over the real origin of a Thanksgiving Day in America," the November 23 article stated. "It seems, however, that the first one was in New-England, established not by Puritans, but by men of the Church of England. In 1607, at Monhegan, near the Kennebeck, a thanksgiving was celebrated."

The article proceeded to proclaim a supposed truth about the meal of choice for the day as well: "And thus, while Thanksgiving Day may be a New-England invention, and, as a national observance may have had its beginning in New-York, the noble turkey, its most glorious feature, was first discovered in the South." (In fact, we now know that the *domestic* turkeys of which we are so fond can trace their lineage back to tamed Aztec birds from southern Mexico.)

Also in 1889, a writer named Jane G. Austin took the tale a step further, publishing an entire novel on the topic, titled *Standish of Standish: A Story of the Pilgrims*. This highly romanticized—and fictionalized—account of the relations between the Native peoples and the Pilgrims, in which Austin described a fanciful outdoor dinner between the two groups, became the inspiration for a *Ladies' Home Journal* article seven years later, which described the perfect Thanksgiving Day dinner. The article included such details from the book as: "roast turkey, dressed with beechnuts . . . rare venison pasties . . . savory meat stews . . . delicious oysters (the gift of the Indians, and the first ever tasted by the white men) . . . great bowls of clam chowder . . ." Salads, baskets overflowing with grapes and nuts, decorated tables, cakes, porridge . . . The story was headed with an illustration by W. L. Taylor, titled *The First Thanksgiving Dinner, with Portraits of the Pilgrim Fathers*.

In 1899, the *Journal of Education*—"Devoted to Education, Science, and Literature"—cited *both* Austin's book and the *Ladies' Home Journal* article in their "Thanksgiving References," claiming that *Standish of Standish* was "worthy of careful study," and that the *Ladies' Home Journal* article was "a very good account of . . . the first Thanksgiving."

Again, it seemed, a women's magazine—not unlike the *Lady's Book*—was influencing, albeit inaccurately, the course of American culture.

Hale may very well have longed for a national day of thanksgiving, but neither she nor Lincoln—nor any other presidential proclamation following in their footsteps—sought to commemorate a specific event that occurred in

New England, or to modify the story of how or what was eaten. Rather, in their eyes, they were merely extending a custom, a tradition, a practice going back so very many years, of taking time to be thankful.

It's true that the intentions of early adopters are often not borne out by subsequent generations of interpretations. If Hale's request was for a unifying holiday, and Lincoln's acquiescence was an attempt to solidify a moment of unification in a fragmented country, neither would have any idea how their actions would combine and evolve later. Never in her life would Hale have envisioned football being part of the national celebration. Lincoln, determined to keep the country together, probably would have thought it strange to imagine department store parades.

In the months following the upended holiday of 1939, various investigations attempted to determine just how much Roosevelt's change in tradition had really helped Christmas sales nationwide, especially in light of how much it had divided the states. And in May 1941, Roosevelt himself admitted the experiment—with the upheaval among states and sports and more—had not been a successful one.

However, there was an enduring result of Roosevelt's failed experiment: In that fall of 1941, the issue Hale had brought to everyone's attention years earlier was finally addressed with decisive action. A House resolution was put forth to make the holiday the *last* Thursday in the month. But a Senate judiciary committee insisted on a change— from the "last" Thursday to the "fourth." The change was quickly accepted in the wake of much more pressing news—the bombing of Pearl Harbor.

As with the president who initially answered Hale's call for a unifying holiday, Roosevelt, too, took the holiday in a more fixed direction and also did so at a time of increasing peril. On December 26, 1941, little more than two weeks after Pearl Harbor and as the United States entered into World War II, Roosevelt signed the thanksgiving resolution with little fanfare. In doing so he established, once and for all, Thanksgiving Day as a federal holiday in the United States of America—seventy-eight years after President Lincoln's initial proclamation of 1863, nearly a century after Sarah Josepha Hale began her campaign for a national holiday on the last Thursday of November.

The festivities Hale envisioned and shared were a reflection of her own upbringing in New England, including the foods and religious observances she had learned from *her* Puritan ancestors. The thanksgivings of the 1860s were a reflection of a nation in the throes of—and finally free of—the shackles of war. For Roosevelt, more than any other president, the holiday was steeped in the undeniable commercialism that had become increasingly associated with the day.

But World War II took its toll on many facets of American life, including the holiday. The Macy's Thanksgiving Day Parade was canceled between 1942 and 1944. Food rations were in place, presenting challenges even for those fortunate enough to celebrate at home. The Thanksgiving cover Norman Rockwell created for the November 1942 *Saturday*

Evening Post depicted an exhausted army cook. Rockwell himself painted a turkey that Thanksgiving Day, but it would not grace the magazine's cover until March 3, 1943. The completed image, of a family gathered around a Thanksgiving table, was titled *Freedom from Want* and was inspired by President Roosevelt's 1941 State of the Union address. In what is often referred to as the "Four Freedoms Speech," Roosevelt described what he saw as the essential freedoms: freedom of speech, freedom of worship, freedom from want, and freedom from fear. Rockwell created images for all of them, which were used to sell an estimated $132 million in war bonds. To illustrate *Freedom from Want*, which accompanied an essay in the *Post* by Filipino American author and activist Carlos Bulosan, Rockwell chose a Thanksgiving meal and used family and friends as his models. A grandmother places a turkey on a table surrounded by generations of guests. It became one of his most popular illustrations ever.

A year later, however, Rockwell could not look away from the suffering abroad. In November 1943, his *Refugee Thanksgiving* cover featured a young Italian girl with long dark hair sitting amid fallen columns, chains, and rubble. Her hands are clasped in prayer, a simple tin pan sits on her knee, and the jacket of an American GI drapes her shoulders.

Even in celebration, the holiday often reflected the solemnity of the moment, in which individuals found even the smallest graces for which to give thanks. *Home for Thanksgiving*, the cover Rockwell created for the November 24, 1945, *Saturday Evening Post*, broadcast the nation's gratitude at the war's end. There were no grand tables or turkey shoots, no

Pilgrims or footballers. Just a mother and a uniformed son sitting together in a simple kitchen peeling potatoes. As models for the cover, Rockwell used Alex Hagelberg and her son Dick, a bombardier who had flown sixty-five successful missions over Germany and had recently returned home safe to celebrate Thanksgiving with his mother.

CHAPTER 14

THE PAIN OF EVOLUTION

Massasoit stood his ground firmly, surrounded by Native peoples. There was no feast. There were no games. There was, however, a ceremony and dancing. Then the gathered Native Americans walked away from Massasoit and proceeded en masse toward the *Mayflower*, which was docked at the wharf. Each person wore a red armband with a single feather. When they reached the vessel, the group of men and women boarded and proceeded to climb the ship's rigging, where high above, two flags flew in the breeze. Those who reached the top of the rigging removed the seventeenth-century English flag. In its place, the group hoisted a banner of blue silk, bearing the image of a red tepee. Shortly after, the group disembarked and made their way to a rock bearing the site's name.

The date was November 23, 1972. The site, Plymouth, Massachusetts. Massasoit, a statue. The occasion, Thanksgiving: a national day of mourning.

The further the country moved away from what had been a common eighteenth- and nineteenth-century practice of issuing a slew of various thanksgiving proclamations—for prayer, fasting, battle victories—the more the thanksgiving celebrated by Americans at the end of November grew in popularity. And with that particular development evolved the notion that one of those early thanksgivings must have come first—and there was a ferocious desire to claim it.

For example, in 1959, the Texas Society of the Daughters of the American Colonists proclaimed Francisco Vázquez de Coronado's 1541 fete on what was now Texas soil the "first thanksgiving," and commemorated it as such. Three years later, after President John F. Kennedy issued *his* Thanksgiving proclamation in 1962—in which he referred to the 1621 event as the first thanksgiving—Senator John J. Wicker of Virginia fired off a telegram to Kennedy, criticizing the Massachusetts native for the claim and asking that the Berkeley Plantation thanksgiving, held in December 1619 by Captain Woodlief, his crew, and settlers, be acknowledged. "Please issue an appropriate correction," the senator wrote.

A year later, on November 5, 1963, President Kennedy dutifully issued a Thanksgiving proclamation one hundred years after Lincoln's. In it, Kennedy lauded our "forefathers in Virginia and Massachusetts," as well as George Washington's first proclamation and Abraham Lincoln's during the Civil War. Virginia was pleased. Kennedy was unable to celebrate the hundredth anniversary of a string of continuous nationally observed thanksgivings. He was assassinated in Dallas just six days before.

The postwar years saw economic booms as well as increased political unrest and activity. Black Power and Red Power movements erupted and brought issues of inequality to the forefront of the national conscience. There were advances and missteps, progress and retraction. The United States had not only become a much more diverse country, many Americans were working to highlight and celebrate that diversity. Yet so many Americans still struggled to see themselves fairly represented in the imagery put forth in advertising and, perhaps more important, in textbooks and schools. Invoking the Pilgrims or Puritans was becoming increasingly loaded. And on March 29, 1964, when minister and activist Malcolm X spoke of the nation's early settlers, he captured a feeling shared by countless disenfranchised individuals living within American borders. "Our forefathers weren't the Pilgrims," he said to a predominantly African American crowd gathered in the upper Manhattan neighborhood of Washington Heights. "We didn't land on Plymouth Rock; the rock was landed on us."

In the turbulent awakening of the sixties, one could sense the struggle of countless communities yearning to be understood and appreciated for their contributions to the American story. In November 1969, the Virginia thanksgiving story of Berkeley Plantation was read into the *Congressional Record*. That same year, Senator Edward "Ted" Kennedy of Massachusetts and the Special Subcommittee on Indian Education issued a report, "Indian Education: A National

Tragedy—A National Challenge." The report examined policy, schooling, and recommendations for bettering the lot of the more than eight hundred thousand Native peoples living in the United States. In his foreword, Kennedy began, "The American vision of itself is of a nation of citizens determining their own destiny; of cultural difference flourishing in an atmosphere of mutual respect; of diverse people shaping their lives and the lives of their children. This subcommittee has undertaken an examination of a major failure in this policy: the education of Indian children." Kennedy called the statistical findings included in the report—from unemployment to infant mortality—a "national disgrace. . . . [T]he 'first American' has become the 'last American.'" The report included "a mandate and a blueprint for change, so that the American Indian can regain his rightful place in our society."

The following year, a group of approximately twenty-five Native peoples went to Plymouth on Thanksgiving and buried its fabled rock under mounds of sand. Not far from that rock stood the ten-foot-tall bronze statue of Massasoit—or Ousamequin—the great sachem, or leader, of the Wampanoag who aided the Pilgrims in their survival. Sculpted by Cyrus E. Dallin, the statue had been erected in 1921 and formally dedicated in 1922, and was to commemorate the three hundredth anniversary of the 1620 landing of the Pilgrims. The group that had commissioned and raised funds for the statue was the Improved Order of Red Men, a fraternal order whose membership was exclusively *white*, but whose rituals, "dress," and terminology were modeled after what white men of the era considered to be the practices of Native peoples. The Pilgrim Society of Plymouth donated the land.

Not everyone was impressed with the proposed statue. In 1920, prior to its dedication, Charlotte L. Mitchell—referred to in the press as Princess Wootonekanuske—was touted by journalists as the *sole* titled descendant of Massasoit alive (though she apparently had living siblings). Then living on just $300 per year, she was interviewed by the *Boston Post* about the bronzed representation of her ancestor. She questioned the intent of the whole enterprise, though she would reluctantly participate in the unveiling. "They erect an attractive statue—a landmark. But gratitude! There's none! The statue lacks real value because it represents nothing. Gratitude!"

More protests at Plymouth followed. And on Thanksgiving of 1972, the United American Indians of New England assembled at Plymouth and protested the holiday that, for many Native Americans, had become a national day of mourning. The statement the group issued was that they were fasting to "mourn the loss of Indian life, and culture," which had begun, for the Native peoples, with the arrival of the Europeans.

The era of protest and social change had apparently made somewhat of an impact on America's politicians—if temporarily. For a brief, shining moment, it appeared as if they were willing to listen. One sign of what might have been potentially shifting times: That same Thanksgiving Day, in Washington, DC, the flag of the Wampanoag flew over the Capitol building.

The following year, 1973, on the Saturday after Thanksgiving, Pilgrim descendent Asa Paine Cobb Lombard Sr. presented that very same flag to eighty-one-year-old Lorenzo

Jeffers—then chief of the Wampanoag people. "For too long," Lombard said, "we have delayed our obligation to these people who made this nation possible." *Mayflower* descendants and Native peoples attended a ceremony during which Jeffers encouraged better understanding of the events that transpired between the Indigenous peoples and the newcomers, saying to the crowd, "This is the only way to create harmony."

Lombard, too, it seemed, desired a better understanding going forward. "When the time comes, and history is not read with prejudice, in the blue above them all will be the name Massasoit, the greatest of all humanitarians. Had it not been for Massasoit . . . I would not be here today."

American culture seemed on the verge of understanding, of making amends.

Two years later, the biggest, most heavily televised thanksgiving celebration in the country—the Macy's Thanksgiving Day Parade—added the Pilgrim Man and Woman to their parade lineup.

During the mid 1970s, as the two hundredth anniversary of the signing of the Declaration of Independence approached, Americans began paying greater attention not just to the colonial era but to the colonization of America in general. This newfound fascination was reflected in annual presidential proclamations.

In 1977, President Jimmy Carter paid tribute to a colonial bicentennial of a different sort: "[I]n 1777, Samuel Adams composed the first National Thanksgiving proclamation, and the Continental Congress called upon the governors of every state to designate a day when all Americans could join together and express their gratitude for God's providence 'with united hearts.'" The following year, Carter mentioned 1621, as well as the Continental Congress.

In 1981, Ronald Reagan reverted to the Pilgrim story, but he managed to mention the contributions of the Native Americans. "After the harvest they gathered their families together and joined in celebration and prayer with the native Americans who had taught them so much. Clearly our forefathers were thankful not only for the material well-being of their harvest but for this abundance of goodwill as well."

Over the past few decades, with the benefit of more expansive knowledge of the history and concerns of the Native community, presidents have had hits and misses in their proclamations—most of which no Americans ever read or hear.

In 1984, Ronald Reagan opened his proclamation by stating, "As we remember the faith and values that made America great, we should recall that our tradition of Thanksgiving is older than our Nation itself. Indeed, the Native American Thanksgivings antedated those of the new Americans. In the words of the eloquent Seneca tradition of the Iroquois, '. . . give it your thought, that with one mind we may now give thanks to Him our Creator.'" He continued: "From the first Pilgrim observance in 1621, to the nine years before and during the American Revolution when the Continental Congress declared days of Fast and Prayer and days of

Thanksgiving, we have turned to Almighty God to express our gratitude for the bounty and good fortune we enjoy as individuals and as a nation. America truly has been blessed."

Reagan cast a wide and not *entirely* accurate net that year: the Iroquois, the Pilgrims, the Continental Congress, and past presidents. Reagan's 1985 proclamation began by acknowledging that "the time and date of the first American thanksgiving observance may be uncertain." He cited events in Maine in 1607, in Virginia in 1619, and among the Dutch and the Spaniards. He then mistakenly stated that Plymouth Colony governor William Bradford proclaimed that special day to "render thanksgiving." There is no evidence of this, and this idea has been particularly difficult to expunge from the American cultural consciousness. Reagan made another significant mention as well, and is the only president to date ever to do so: "Although there were many state and national thanksgiving days proclaimed in the ensuing years," he wrote, "it was the tireless crusade of one woman, Sarah Josepha Hale, that finally led to the establishment of this beautiful feast as an annual nationwide observance."

Three years later, in 1988, he stated: "The images of the Thanksgiving celebrations at America's earliest settlement—of Pilgrim and Iroquois Confederacy assembled in festive friendship—resonate with even greater power in our own day."

The acknowledgment of the Iroquois Confederacy (if not the Wampanoag specifically) was still significant, as the Haudenosaunee—as that six-nation confederation is also called—inspired the U.S. Constitution. In 1751, Benjamin Franklin wrote in a letter to his printing partner James

Parker, saying that "securing the Friendship of the Indians is of the greatest Consequence to these Colonies. . . ." He saw a need for the English colonies to work together, and did not feel they were moving in the right direction. He cited the Iroquois Confederacy and their constitution—founded upon the Great Law of Peace—as an example of a union among six nations that had lasted ages and still appeared "indissoluble."

The Haudenosaunee Confederacy employs a bundle of arrows as a symbolic representation of unity. Franklin and the other members of the Continental Congress would later take that symbol as inspiration as well, when creating the seal of the United States of America: Thirteen arrows are shown to symbolize the new union of the thirteen colonies. And in 1987, in preparation for the bicentennial of the U.S. Constitution, there was finally a formal congressional acknowledgment of the Haudenosaunee influence on the United States government.

"If Americans are going to celebrate the anniversary of their Constitution," Chief Oren Lyons, an Onondaga and former associate professor of American studies at the State University of New York at Buffalo, told the *New York Times*, "we figure we had better tell them where the idea came from."

But even with these attempts at atonement and acknowledgments of the numerous contributions of the Native American community, the mythology of the thanksgiving story stuck, from George H. W. Bush through Bill Clinton, who, in 1995, was the first president to mention the Wampanoag by name, writing: "In 1621, Massachusetts Bay Governor William Bradford invited members of the neighboring

Wampanoag tribe to join the Pilgrims as they celebrated their first harvest in a new land. This 3-day festival brought people together to delight in the richness of the earth and to give praise for their new friendships and progress."

Though the Clinton proclamation strikes an upbeat tone, there is no evidence that Bradford issued any such invitation.

In November 2001, George W. Bush invoked Pilgrims, Eisenhower, Lincoln, and Washington. In 2005, he took a more general, encompassing approach and celebrated "explorers and settlers."

In 2009, President Barack Obama went further in acknowledging the contributions of the Native peoples in his proclamations, and largely what he penned was historically accurate: "What began as a harvest celebration between European settlers and indigenous communities nearly four centuries ago has become our cherished tradition of Thanksgiving. . . . We also recognize the contributions of Native Americans, who helped the early colonists survive their first harsh winter and continue to strengthen our Nation."

Then, in 2010, Obama alluded to the once and continuing contributions of the Native Americans: "A beloved American tradition, Thanksgiving Day offers us the opportunity to focus our thoughts on the grace that has been extended to our people and our country. This spirit brought together the newly arrived Pilgrims and the Wampanoag tribe—who had been living and thriving around Plymouth, Massachusetts, for thousands of years—in an autumn harvest feast centuries ago. This Thanksgiving Day, we re-flect on the compassion and contributions of Native Ameri-cans, whose skill in agriculture helped the early colonists survive, and whose rich culture continues to add to our Na-tion's heritage. We also pause our normal pursuits on this day and join in a spirit of fellowship and gratitude for the year's bounties and blessings."

He echoed these thoughts again in 2011: "One of our Na-tion's oldest and most cherished traditions, Thanksgiving Day brings us closer to our loved ones and invites us to re-flect on the blessings that enrich our lives. The observance recalls the celebration of an autumn harvest centuries ago, when the Wampanoag tribe joined the Pilgrims at Plymouth Colony to share in the fruits of a bountiful season. The feast honored the Wampanoag for generously extending their knowledge of local game and agriculture to the Pilgrims, and today we renew our gratitude to all American Indians and Alaska Natives. We take this time to remember the ways that the First Americans have enriched our Nation's heri-tage, from their generosity centuries ago to the everyday contributions they make to all facets of American life. As we come together with friends, family, and neighbors to cele-brate, let us set aside our daily concerns and give thanks for the providence bestowed upon us."

Although it is nice to think that the feast "honored" the Wampanoag, there is no evidence they were even intended guests. However, President Obama made serious strides by drawing attention specifically to the invaluable contributions of the Native peoples to America—not their perceived role in someone else's seasonal pageant. And in his Every Student Succeeds Act, Obama included the requirement that any educational agency seeking Title I grant funding needed to consult with representatives of Native nations as they developed their curricula.

Between 2017 and 2019, President Donald Trump, in his proclamations, mentioned the Pilgrims, the Wampanoag, George Washington, and Abraham Lincoln's role in the evolution of the holiday. He, too, like most of his predecessors, erred in claiming that Bradford "proclaimed" that thanksgiving.

In 2017, it was announced that Ousamequin's remains and associated objects—along with those of forty-two other burials—would be reinterred near their original burial site of Burr's Hill, Rhode Island, in what is now Warren. Thanks to the Native American Graves Protection and Repatriation Act, passed in 1990, Native nations could reclaim the remains and possessions of their ancestors that were held by federal institutions, such as the Smithsonian National Museum of the American Indian in Washington, DC. The process of gathering artifacts related to the life of Ousamequin took more than twenty years.

Some schools today are doing a better job of telling the story of seventeenth-century America and the Native Americans, but there's so much more work to be done. We seem to have lost much of the ground that was gained in the 1970s. Today, the U.S. Mint still calls 1621 the first thanksgiving and even issued a coin honoring the 1621 treaty between the Pilgrims and the Wampanoag—a treaty that was cast aside, with bloodshed and centuries of genocide to follow.

=====

The California-raised food writer and gustatory philosopher M. F. K. Fisher celebrated not just the transcendent experience of cooking and eating but also the significance of the ceremony that often surrounded even the simplest of meals. She acknowledged that at holiday gatherings, Thanksgiving included, it is "almost too easy" to pour on the sentiment, and that coming together to give thanks is often much more complicated and anxiety inducing. "The cold truth is that family dinners are more often than not an ordeal of nervous indigestion, preceded by hidden resentment and ennui and accompanied by psychosomatic jitters." This saddened and appalled her, because she knew just how joyful a good meal with loved ones could be. She clung to that vision, and shared it for the rest of her days, proselytizing that "there is communion of more than our bodies when bread is broken and wine drunk."

In recent years, the holiday has evolved in so many ways, from "friendsgiving" to vegan turkey. Hosting Thanksgiving is, for many, a rite of passage, a sign of one's maturity and growing munificence. The first time you cooked. The first attempt to carve or give a toast in front of an audience. The first time you spoke in front of others, announcing that for which you were thankful. For many newcomers arriving in America, joining in a Thanksgiving meal or preparing one's own is a part of adjusting to the new culture. And, one might add, ridiculing the mythology surrounding the sanitized notions of that "first thanksgiving" has itself become commonplace at many tables.

Presidential proclamations, in some cases, have evolved, as well. More important, our population has evolved, as has—to a limited extent—our understanding of sorrowful past events on this continent and countless others across the globe.

Perhaps it is time for the holiday to take one great step forward and evolve once more into its most inclusive and gracious form yet. A holiday all Americans can feel good to be thankful for.

From fasting and humiliation to gluttony and thanks, for battle victories and good harvests, from the secular to the religious and everywhere in between, one thing that emerges from all the thanksgiving flavors we've sampled over the years: There was no "first." And if the holiday is to be a reflection of who Americans—all Americans—are, there is one element only that has, and must, remain unchanged through the centuries and across time, continents, and shifting political climates. One element above all:

Gratitude.

CHAPTER 15

CHOOSE GRATITUDE

A minister, a rabbi, and an imam walk into an apse . . .
One of the oldest continuously ministering churches
in the United States is Marble Collegiate in lower
Manhattan, New York City, founded in 1628 in what was
then the Dutch colony of New Amsterdam. The first sermons were preached in a gristmill. At the time, the population of New Amsterdam was estimated to be roughly three
hundred. In 1854, a new church was built near a dairy farm
in the distant, far northern reaches of town—way up on
Twenty-Ninth Street. The Neo-Romanesque Gothic structure had a 215-foot steeple and a facade of Tuckahoe marble,
giving the church its name. The church has seen much history pass through and by its doors, both joyous and somber
in tone, from holiday celebrations to the funeral procession
of Abraham Lincoln.

Now, nearly four hundred years, many renovations, and several historic designations later, Marble Collegiate Church not only still stands but continues to hold services, and hosts the occasional tourist. The church describes itself as a "diverse, inclusive community" and welcomes people of all faiths as well as those who don't practice any one in particular.

On Thanksgiving Day in 1991—the year of the Persian Gulf War—the church, under the direction of Dr. Arthur Caliandro, launched its annual "trialogue," in which a leader of the Jewish and the Muslim communities each joined the minister for a joint sermon. The annual tradition continues to this day, though the date varies. Interfaith dialogues and sermons like these happen all over the country, many of them during Thanksgiving weekend, many taking an ecumenical or nondenominational approach, and very many becoming celebratory and illuminating litanies on that which all humans have in common.

The unifying theme among so many communities, secular and religious, is one of the power of gratitude. More than simply the trend of the moment, the topic of gratitude as a health benefit has gained serious momentum in recent years. The timeless, global practice of gratitude is now enjoying an increasing amount of positive attention.

As Americans assess their present roles in their own community, as well as in the global one, they can move in the direction of an increasingly diverse and ideally aware culture. Embracing gratitude can play a key role for Americans seeking authentic ways to best carry this annual tradition forward. Beyond any spirit of the season, bringing "thanksgiving" into one's daily life is linked to improved mental and even physical health, and it continues to benefit from a growing body of neuroscientific and psychological research.

Setting aside a dedicated time to stop and say thank you—whether aloud, to oneself, or to another—for even the smallest things in life has been proved to benefit one's health in numerous ways. Even minor gratitude practice has been linked to the reduction of, for example, cellular inflammation and anxiety; the lessening of symptoms related to aches, pains, and other illnesses; the lowering of blood pressure; and the boosting of the immune system. In studies, participants reported feeling better physically and mentally, and credited cultivating an attitude of gratitude with reducing symptoms related to depression. And while gratitude practice decreases those, it can also *increase* positive, beneficial feelings such as self-esteem, appreciation, and mental fortitude. As an added bonus, gratitude as a regular practice can promote better, sounder sleep.

The simple act of writing down things for which one is thankful—i.e., gratitude journaling—not only engenders more of that good feeling in the people doing the writing but can also impact their relationships, improving their capacity to both experience and exhibit empathy when dealing with others. The practice, in that sense, pays it forward.

Studies supporting these findings keep adding up. In 2010, researchers Randy A. Sansone, a psychiatrist and professor, and Lori A. Sansone, a family medicine doctor, surveyed a large body of research conducted with a variety of populations, including adolescents, high school athletes, and college students, illustrating the "association between gratitude and an overall sense of well-being."

For the purposes of the paper, the pair defined gratitude as "the appreciation of what is valuable and meaningful to oneself; it is a general state of thankfulness and/or appreciation." The crux of that definition is "meaningful to oneself." There are many ways, big and small, to be grateful, but what is taken for granted by one person may be reason for extreme gratitude for another. The assessment of gratitude is deeply personal; each individual experiences it in different, though equally empowering, ways.

Psychologist and professor Robert Emmons at the University of California, Davis, and Michael McCullough, director of the Evolution and Human Behavior Laboratory and professor of psychology at the University of Miami, have established themselves as leading researchers in the field of gratitude. In a 2003 report, the pair described a study of a group of undergraduate students. They divided the subjects into three groups and collected ten weekly reports in which participants listed either (1) things for which they were thankful, (2) things that were "hassles," or (3) "events"—more neutral happenings. Emmons and McCullough also asked each group to report on their mood and physical well-being. The researchers noted that "the effect on positive affect appeared to be the most robust finding," and that the "conscious focus on blessings may have emotional and interpersonal benefits."

In 2017, psychology professors Joel Wong and Joshua Brown of Indiana University reported the results of a study they conducted with three hundred adults, many of them college students, and all of whom were already seeking psychological counseling for depression and anxiety. The study did not replace the psychological counseling. Wong and Brown simply instructed one group of study participants to write a letter of gratitude to someone each week for three weeks. The second group was instructed to journal about any negative feelings that they were having. The third, control group had no writing assignment and simply attended counseling sessions.

Despite the short time frame during which the students were observed—three weeks—the students who wrote letters of gratitude exhibited the greatest improvement in symptoms of all three groups. Following these students after the initial three weeks, Wong and Brown found evidence that the positive mental health effects the participants experienced were evident as much as twelve weeks out. In fact, they "accrued over time." Students who wrote letters were not required to mail them; it turned out that the mere act of cataloging that for which they were grateful had a positive effect all on its own. The impact was not just that they were then able to focus on the good but also that the gratitude practice could somehow help "shift . . . focus away from negative feelings and thoughts."

If the proof is in the pudding, the pudding in this case is the gray matter. Three months after the initial psychotherapy sessions, doctors took fMRIs of the letter-writing group and the therapy-only group as they performed what was called a "pay it forward" task. A functional MRI (magnetic resonance imaging) shows the metabolism of oxygen within brain cells, allowing doctors to see which areas are stimulated—or "light up"—under different circumstances.

The two groups were given money by a fictional benefactor and then asked to pass the funds on to someone if they felt moved by gratitude to do so. Participants were polled on how much money, if any, they passed along. They were also asked how grateful they felt toward the benefactor, how much they wanted to help their chosen charity, and how appreciative, in general, they felt about their lives—as well as how guilty they might feel if they did not pass along the funds.

The fMRI results showed that the brain activity of those who gave out of gratitude was markedly different from those who gave out of a sense of obligation or guilt. The scientists could see increased activity and neural sensitivity in the medial prefrontal cortex—the brain's decision-making and learning hub—of the grateful students. It was almost as if the "gratitude state of mind" had rewired their brains. "This suggests that people who are more grateful are also more attentive to how they express gratitude," concluded Wong and Brown. "[S]imply expressing gratitude may have lasting effects on the brain."

Recent research has linked gratitude with a tendency toward generosity. The key lies in the ventromedial prefrontal cortex in the brain's frontal lobe, which has been shown to be stimulated by altruistic activity. Researchers from the University of Oregon's Emotions and Neuroplasticity Project in the Department of Psychology mapped the brain activity of participants as they reacted to the stimulus of money deposited into their *own* accounts, as opposed to money deposited into those of a charity. There was hard synaptic evidence: The brain itself connected thankfulness practice with altruistic action. According to project director Christina M. Karns, as reported in *ScienceDaily* in 2017, "[P]eople who reported more altruistic and grateful traits showed a reward-related brain response when the charity received money that was larger than when they received the money themselves." Gratitude journaling enhanced these results.

And humans are apparently not the only altruistic animals on the planet. A report titled "The Science of Gratitude," prepared for the John Templeton Foundation by the Greater Good Science Center at UC Berkeley, cites research suggesting that animals such as fish and, ironically, vampire bats exhibit "reciprocal altruism," helping others of their species even if it does no immediate good—or possibly even does harm—to themselves. Social and cultural factors play into the gratitude experience, of course, but there is mounting evidence that doing good for others is associated with doing good for oneself.

When you take the time and make the effort to feel thankful during trying times, the impact of gratitude is often strongest. The UC Berkeley report stated, "Several studies have found that more grateful people experience less depression and are more resilient following traumatic events."

More support for this idea comes from a study on the post–September 11, 2001, terrorist attacks in New York City, which was published in the *Journal of Personality and*

Social Psychology. Researchers found that seeking reasons to be thankful in the midst of agony and sadness was a key factor in what they referred to as a person's "bouncebackability."

This particular quality—resilience—has also been studied by Dr. Emmons at UC Davis, who has researched gratitude for nearly two decades: "[N]ot only will a grateful attitude help," he wrote in 2013, "it is *essential*. In fact, it is precisely under crisis conditions when we have the most to gain by a grateful perspective on life."

Emmons writes that remembering the hard times can offer inspiration for appreciating the present. In a sense, we literally have to see where we've been in order to value where we are. Emmons notes that practicing gratitude does not mean ignoring or devaluing the pain and difficulty that life often brings our way. Feelings are what they are—messy, often unpleasant, and impossible to control. Gratitude, on the other hand, is an active choice, and many neuroscientists and psychiatric professionals are finding that choosing gratitude really is as good for the body as it may be for the soul.

Humans through time often gave thanks after living through a difficult ordeal: a lack of food, a harrowing journey, a trying personal loss. More than merely looking on the bright side of things, gratitude practice was and is a conscious shift of focus, the deliberate application of a different lens through which to view what was otherwise an unpleasant experience. It is beneficial for gratitude to be "chosen in spite of one's situation or circumstances," Emmons writes.

We don't have to look far to see this very dynamic in the

story of the national holiday of Thanksgiving in the United States.

Sarah Josepha Hale's commitment to her writing and desire to create an annual, codified holiday centered around thankfulness came on the heels of the sudden loss of her husband and the need to support her five small children. Abraham Lincoln's decision to support Hale's bid to establish the holiday came in the middle of the Civil War, at a time when he routinely walked past the increasing number of graves being dug beyond the doors of his cottage at the Soldiers' Home. It came at a time when families north and south were torn apart by political differences. It came at a time when things seemed darkest, and yet in that first presidential proclamation of thanksgiving that Lincoln issued— even as he acknowledged the difficulties and trials that the country was experiencing—he chose to offer reasons, many of them, for everyone, on all sides, to be thankful.

The concept is dead simple. Write a thank-you note. Mentally send sentiments of thanks to someone far away. Keep the increasingly popular gratitude journal. There is no best or right way to practice gratitude. Humans have been giving thanks to deities and spirits and nature and friends and family and fate and providence and more for as long as *Homo sapiens* has paced the earth.

Much like the ceremony, day, or dinner of thanksgiving itself, there is no perfect way to celebrate, either. Nor is there a need for that celebration to be based on any one event. Gratitude, culturally and historically, is so significant and formidable on its own that it can be celebrated anytime. And in seasonal concert with that, there is value in the practice and tradition of all of us coming together in thanksgiving on that sentiment's namesake day. And that value can be perpetually reaped, like so many harvests past.

Gratitude and celebrations of thanks have taken many forms over the centuries, many of them culturally and politically varied. We have choices about how we decide to bequeath this tradition to future generations. What is next for the national Thanksgiving? What messages—and the intentions behind them—are we choosing to pass on?

There are developments in this arena that Hale might well smile at, were she here to witness them. If anything, American culture has developed countless ways to promote giving and reflection. #GivingTuesday is now an annual charitable campaign that takes place the Tuesday after Thanksgiving and helps to balance out the commercialism we still see on full display that holiday weekend. November is also Native American Heritage Month. And some of the oldest, most lasting, and inspirationally tolerant instruction on giving thanks can be traced to the traditions of the original inhabitants of the North American continent. Ironically, some of the best teachers of the concept of gratitude are members of the very community that is most often maligned by the pat, simplistic thanksgiving story trotted out during the season.

Throughout the customs and histories of Indigenous peoples, we find not only examples of how to give thanks but also an understanding that it is something that should be practiced daily.

If the nation is to continue to evolve into its better self, the best part of the holiday should offer a way forward that reflects the best part of the American people.

It's intriguing to ponder what a crusading editor like Hale might write in the *Lady's Book* about the celebration of thanksgiving today and how that celebration has transformed over time. Imagine if during the week of Thanksgiving, more schools across the nation dedicated instruction about the role Indigenous peoples and their heritage and culture have played in the founding, growth, and strengthening of the United States. Picture classroom projects focused on learning about a nearby Native community or performing an act of charity. Envision that holiday week focused on the longstanding traditions of appreciation and thanks that permeate all religions and cultures around the globe.

The day after Thanksgiving is Native American Heritage Day. Thanksgiving remains a time of mourning for many Native peoples. Let us share with the nation's children the reasons such a day exists. Let us encourage local school boards to create new, inclusive, inspiring lesson plans to teach the holiday in partnership with Native communities. The resources available to families and teachers are countless and readily available. Above all, encourage kids to come up with something on their own—they're often better at that than we give them credit for.

Let's allow execution and action to reflect the best of our intentions. In so many ways, the practice of gratitude—whether on Thanksgiving Day or any other day—becomes a question of intention. Hale's intention—to create unity through a shared experience of thankfulness—required lifelong dedication and her ability to remain resolute despite constant disappointment. But she rarely framed it that way. As much of the research suggests, gratitude can be a framework. For every president who refused her plea to establish a national holiday of thanksgiving, Hale routinely heralded the governors and diplomats and other community leaders who *did* agree with her. For every personal loss, she sought a new way to move forward—and bring others along with her. Hale never silenced her true voice, and often raised that voice in the service of others.

To take thanksgiving back, to take it forward, we can choose to reflect the very spirit Hale embodied throughout her long life. We can exhibit the best of ourselves.

"We are not enemies, but friends. We must not be enemies," Lincoln said in his first inaugural address. "Though passion may have strained, it must not break our bonds of affection. The mystic chords of memory . . . will yet swell . . . when again touched, as surely they will be, by the better angels of our nature."

The uninterrupted string of annual thanksgiving celebrations that began nearly 160 years ago, thanks to Hale's relentless efforts and Lincoln's recognition of her vision, has since changed in new and complex ways. But we are poised to manifest this holiday rooted in thanks and encourage it to evolve once again.

What has become such an integral part of American culture should continue to grow to reflect that culture and the best parts of itself. Appreciation. Inclusion. Compassion. Celebration. Charity.

Let today begin a revolution of gratitude, and grace.

EPILOGUE

Y ou eat my raccoon, you'll throw that turkey away."
I have my doubts, but the seventy-five-year-old
master oyster roaster is very convincing. It is dusk and
we are on an island off the coast of South Carolina, standing
near an inlet. This is the Low Country, a deliciously moody,
tradition-drenched area whose humidity is exceeded only by
its residents' passion for food. My culinary guide stokes the
open fire beneath what looks like tin roofing; tosses fresh
oysters on top; covers them with a wet burlap sack; and lets
water, flame, and tradition work its magic for about ten minutes. A shucking blade unleashes hot, smoky, meaty orbs
that require nothing more than a hearty slurp and ample
napkins. "Away from your body," he instructs my husband,
who is in danger of shish-kebabbing his own gallbladder with
the business end of the knife.

I had asked the oyster maestro what he ate for Thanksgiving. "Raccoon. Squirrel. Rabbit," he answered. Earlier in his

life, there was little money, but you still had to eat. He doesn't need to scrimp that way today, but tradition and taste buds win the day. He likes what he likes. "You can still live off the land," he reminds me. The African American chef's family has been here for generations, and beneath his straw cowboy hat is a face that could pass for sixty. He boasts that his doctors ask him the key to his vitality. He shares that secret with me: tasks that were a part of his daily routine. "I work every day," he says first, firmly believing that sitting too still for too long never does anyone any good. Other daily musts are praying, seventy-five push-ups every morning—sometimes more at night—and, lastly, he tells me, "Say thank you."

I am still on the fence about the raccoon, but this I believe.

He hands me an open oyster and tosses the dripping burlap sack on top of the latest batch of bivalves. Steam rises up into the night air, wafting over a timeless landscape, carrying the scent of charred fish out over the waters from whence they came, a sea that seems, right here and now, teeming with plenty.

But now, let us return to Rome.

During the 2017 Advent season, Pope Francis said, "Joy, prayer, and gratitude are three attitudes that prepare us to live Christmas in an authentic way." Whether Catholic, Jewish, atheist, Muslim, or none of the above, having an "attitude of gratitude" has become, well, a sort of universal beatitude.

When that same pope toured the United States in 2015, he addressed a crowd gathered in New York City's St. Patrick's Cathedral, with these, among other, reflections:

"Joy springs from a grateful heart," he said. "Truly, we have received much, so many graces, so many blessings, and we rejoice in this. It will do us good to think back on our lives with the grace of remembrance. Let us seek the grace of remembrance. . . . To seek the grace of remembrance so as to grow in the spirit of gratitude. Perhaps we need to ask ourselves: are we good at counting our blessings?"

And the pope's last public act in 2019 was in part, and traditionally, a "Te Deum in thanksgiving for the past year."

In the spring of 2020, however, an altogether different, highly unusual scene unfolded in Vatican City.

Pope Francis preached to an empty piazza in front of St. Peter's Basilica. He stood alone in the rain, his arms outstretched, praying to a vacant expanse of cobblestones, a piazza that would under any other circumstances have been swarming with thousands of religious pilgrims. But these were not normal circumstances, not for anyone in Rome, or for that matter, the world over.

I discussed this new world via Skype with Italian friends in Rome not long after the pope's solemn, solitary address. The irony was not lost on me: I was wrapping up a book titled *We Gather Together* just as the phrase "social distancing" was establishing a strong and saddening foothold in the English language. Adding to the required physical isolation so many have endured, painful emotional challenges have at once divided and united Americans as we confront again, with a renewed strength and fervor, the systemic stronghold hate and intolerance continue to have on our culture. These dual pandemics have, as many crises do, thrown into sharp relief not only that which saddens, frustrates, and angers our souls, but that which ultimately has the power to uplift them.

Completing a book about unity and gratitude and the shifting expressions of each over the centuries proved at once soothing and unnerving for me, and my feelings surrounding the topic grew even stronger, if my relationship to the material bobbed and weaved amid this viral bout. If you can't step into the same river twice, neither can you stroll through the pages of the same book in the same manner more than once. A reader brings herself anew to the material with each encounter, and that self is an evolving culmination of experiences and circumstances. And boy, did circumstances get turned on their ear during my experience with the book you're currently reading.

Even during the time that elapsed between finishing a first draft and getting into final proofs, gratitude had taken on new momentum. #GivingTuesday—recently and traditionally the Tuesday after Thanksgiving—was reborn on May 5, amid the coronavirus outbreak. This aspect of the changing times felt familiar and reminded me of one of the motivations behind my desire to write this book: the human tendency toward charity and gratitude in times of crisis and turmoil. It has never felt clearer to me.

I have been happily, if not surprisingly, struck by countless inspirations I witnessed daily during the pandemic. These acts range from the small to the grand, from the local to the global. There are big, beautiful noises, like celebrity chef José Andrés and his World Central Kitchen charity working to feed those who are hungry and suffering—while many of his own restaurants are ostensibly shuttered. And there are quieter actions that cause reverberations just as powerful, like Captain Tom Moore, a ninety-nine-year-old World War II veteran doing laps with a walker in his back-yard in England. Hoping to raise £1,000 by his one hundredth birthday for the National Health Service as it battled the pandemic, Moore inspired donations of more than $40 million by the time this book went to press, and his actions earned him a knighthood from Queen Elizabeth II, to boot.

The media is awash in countless guides to gratitude practice in the midst of crisis, from the practical to-dos to spiritual contemplations: "living gratefully during coronavirus," "practicing gratitude in a time of uncertainty and unrest," "beat the coronavirus blues," "how to keep the greater good in mind" during the pandemic, article titles such as "Activism, Celebrations, and Gratitude Ease Political Angst," and so much more—lists, guides, meditations, podcasts. There is planned giving and spontaneous sharing. Social media posts are chock-full of images of shuttered buildings and sidewalks covered in colorful messages of hope, solidarity, and inspiration. Someone dashing off a message of joy for no one in particular may well bring a smile to people on the other side of the globe. That which is forcing us to keep our distance is enabling our best efforts to bring us together.

If a topic resonates with a writer, won't let that writer go, then that topic must be explored. This book, more than any other I have written, has me wondering how it will read when it is released. Will Hale's belief in the unifying power of thankfulness ring as true now? I cannot know. This book is not intended "for me"; however, I can't stop thinking about what a thanksgiving will look like this year *for me*, as well as for others. Will I enjoy a table full of friends and food? Or might I be attending a "Zoomsgiving," downing turkey and stuffing in front of a computer? Will I be wiping gravy from a mask? Wielding my drumstick with nitrile gloves?

One thing will endure, whether I am carving for a crowd or nibbling in front of a monitor: There will be, as there has always been, gratitude at that feast. For so much, and even for the smallest thing that caused a smile to cross my face.

However you celebrate the day, and its meaning, I know that I will be doing this: closing my eyes, quietly or loudly stating that for which I am most thankful, no matter how sideways things seem to have gone. I will embrace that which can and should always be in ample supply, a timeless practice, which brings us together in spirit if not in person.

ACKNOWLEDGMENTS

Thanking those who have been invaluable to the publication of a book takes on a whole other level of import when the topic of that book is gratitude. As with any other human attempt at offering appreciation, I hope my sincere intentions will outweigh any accidental omissions.

Getting this work out into what has become a very unpredictable world has made it more challenging, but in the process, it has also made me all the more grateful for the tremendous team that made it possible.

This book would not exist without the expertise and support of many individuals and institutions. My agent of more years than either of us would care to admit, Yfat Reiss Gendell, is part sounding board, part truth-telling voice of reason, and full-time advocate. She rests on no laurels—though she could have a comfy bed if she decided to do so—and works tirelessly to help me navigate what is a constantly changing and often volatile industry. Her insights and friendship are of monumental importance to me. She and her team at YRG Partners are a delightfully brilliant, unique bunch, and I feel very fortunate to be on their roster. I am grateful to editor John Parsley for his enthusiasm for this story, and for diving in with voracious energy and verve on this, our maiden publishing voyage together. He was ably assisted by Cassidy Sachs and the rest of the gang at my new home, Dutton and Penguin Random House, including Dutton publisher Christine Ball and president Ivan Held. They never wavered in their support of my book. The managing editorial and production team headed by Susan Schwartz and Linda Rosenberg, including production editor Claire Winecoff, production manager Erin Byrne, and copy editor Martha Schwartz, asked all the right questions and, more important, cleaned up my mistakes when I could not see them anymore. The publicity and marketing crew—including Amanda Walker, Sarah Thegeby, Stephanie Cooper, and Caroline Payne—had their work cut out for them during a pandemic to ensure this book found the right audience. Layout designer Nancy Resnick gave my words a lovely setting on the page; and cover designer Vi-An Nguyen wrapped it up in the cleanest, most enticing package I could ever want. This book would not have been possible without the countless manuscripts, letters, and other archives that provided a peek into the past. The efforts of universities, research libraries, and private foundations to make their work available digitally has been a boon not only to people like me but also to everyone—teachers, students, citizens—who were unable to venture out into the world freely this year. Their contributions are detailed in the Selected Notes and

ACKNOWLEDGMENTS

Sources. On occasion, I need an extra pair of boots on the ground when I cannot be everywhere at once. I thank the intrepid Deirdre Cossman in New York, and my West Coast arm, Drake Witham. My personal support system is vast, and there are too many friends and family to thank for giving me a shot of perspective or bourbon. However, I must call out Lauren Harr and Caroline Green Christopoulos, my always-available, go-to gals of the publicity team at Gold Leaf Literary. My "home" bookstore, the incomparable Malaprop's Bookstore/Cafe in downtown Asheville, North Carolina—I could not ask for a better place to offer my books, host my events, or spend my free time. Abbott Kahler's talent as a writer and generous spirit as a friend keep me (moderately) sane. And finally, I can never thank my husband, Joseph D'Agnese, enough, for serving as in-house editor, expert anxiety reliever, and all-around exceptional human being. Thank you all for seeing this through with me.

SELECTED NOTES AND SOURCES

In the interest of economy, and given that many of these individuals and themes are present across multiple chapters, I have grouped selected key sources by topic, and additional materials by chapter. If I have specifically mentioned the origin of a quote in the text—a verse of the Bible, for example—I have not repeated that information here. Also, if a particular fact is widely known, easily found, and extensively documented—as in one of Malcolm X's most famous quotes, or who shot Abraham Lincoln—I have not included it here. Where applicable, I have added a few insights and notes that might not have made it into the final version of the text. The following sources are substantial but by no means exhaustive.

GLOBAL NOTES

Sarah Josepha Hale's existing papers are scattered across numerous institutions. However, some of the best details about her life came from her own writing, especially the introductions and notes she included in her own books, notably *The Ladies' Wreath*. Her key texts are, especially: *The Ladies' Wreath; A Selection from the Female Poetic Writers of England and America* (Boston: Marsh, Capen & Lyon, 1837); *Northwood; or, A Tale of New England*, vol. 1 and 2 (Boston: Bowles & Dearborn, 1827); *Northwood; or, Life North and South: Showing the True Character of Both*, 2nd ed. (New York: H. Long and Brother, 1852); *Liberia; or, Mr. Peyton's Experiments* (New York: Harper & Brothers, 1853); *Woman's Record; or, Sketches of All Distinguished Women, from "The Beginning" till A.D. 1850,*

Arranged in Four Eras, with Selections from Female Writers of Every Age (New York: Harper & Brothers, 1853); *Manners; or, Happy Homes and Good Society All the Year Round* (Boston: J. E. Tilton, 1868).

There are three primary biographies of Hale: Ruth E. Finley, *The Lady of Godey's: Sarah Josepha Hale* (Philadelphia: J. B. Lippincott, 1931); Sherbrooke Rogers, *Sarah Josepha Hale: A New England Pioneer, 1788–1879* (Grantham, NH: Tompson & Rutter, 1985); Norma R. Fryatt, *Sarah Josepha Hale: The Life and Times of a Nineteenth-Century Career Woman* (New York: Hawthorn Books, 1975).

In 1917, many of Hale's letters were sold at auction. I was thrilled to track down a copy of that catalog, which included letter recipients (Poe, etc.) and quotes: *Letters to Mrs. Sarah Josepha Hale and Maj.-Gen. David Hunter and Other Rare Autographs*, auction catalog No. 1270, Jan. 25–26, 1917 (New York: Anderson Galleries, 1917). Along with the above catalog, perhaps my favorite find was Hale's last will and testament, written in her own hand: Pennsylvania, Wills and Probate Records, 1683–1993, Wills no. 451–491, 1879.

Godey's Lady's Book went by the following titles between 1830 and 1898: *The Lady's Book, Godey's Lady's Book and Ladies' American Magazine, Godey's Magazine and Lady's Book, Godey's Lady's Book, Godey's Lady's Book and Magazine, Godey's Lady's Book* (yet again), and *Godey's Magazine*.

Thanks to organizations such as HathiTrust Digital Library (https://www.hathitrust.org), issues of *Godey's Lady's Book*—including Hale's editorials—can be read in their (scanned) original context. Flowing through the color images of the fashion plates and looking at the cover art and illustrations is also a treat. I am also the delighted owner of a bound edition of all of *Godey's Lady's Book* from 1863. It is a treasure.

Other information sources about Hale's life and family include—but are not limited to: Richardson Wright, "The Madonna in Bustles," in *Forgotten Ladies: Nine Portraits from the American Family Album* (Philadelphia: J. B. Lippincott, 1928); "Death of William G. Hale," *New Orleans Republican*, Jan. 14, 1876.

There is a fair amount of modern-day criticism of Hale, including of her writing and her attitudes toward suffrage and slavery. As I keep my narrative in the moment, as opposed to stopping to provide an overview of such criticism, some may nevertheless find these interesting reads, and it is always useful to view individuals within a present-day context, as it can help inform the past: Patricia Okker, *Our Sister Editors: Sarah J. Hale and the Tradition of Nineteenth-Century American Women Editors* (Athens: University of Georgia Press, 1995); Beverly Peterson, "Mrs. Hale on Mrs. Stowe and Slavery," *American Periodicals* 8 (1998): 30–44, accessed via JSTOR; Nicole Tonkovich Hoffman, "Sarah Josepha Hale (1788–1874 [sic])," *Legacy* 7, no. 2 (Fall 1990): 47–55, accessed via JSTOR; Etsuko Taketani, "Postcolonial Liberia: Sarah Josepha Hale's Africa," *American Literary History* 14, no. 3 (2002): 479–504, accessed via JSTOR; "An *ALH* Forum: 'Race and Antebellum Literature,'" Special Issue, *American Literary History* 14, no. 3 (2002), accessed via JSTOR; L. E. Preston, "Speakers for Women's Rights in Pennsylvania," *Western Pennsylvania Historical Magazine* 54, no. 3 (July 1971): 245–63.

Hale's editorials have been entered and collected in various locations, some as e-books, some as lists. Pilgrim Hall Museum (https://pilgrimhall .org) is a wonderful place to peruse those and other documents related to thanksgiving.

All presidential proclamations and a wide assortment of other presidential documents can be found via a number of sources, including the "Presidential Documents Guide" at the National Archives (https://www .archives.gov/presidential-libraries/research/guide.html), the presidential libraries for each individual president, and the Library of Congress. The Presidency section of the Miller Center of Public Affairs at the University of Virginia (https://millercenter.org/the-presidency) is a fantastic resource with biographical profiles, oral histories, speeches, impeachment proceedings, "Secret White House Tapes"—you name it. My favorite source for one-stop presidential document shopping is the American Presidency Project (https://www.presidency.ucsb.edu/documents) at the University of California, Santa Barbara. It features a searchable database of everything from eulogies to state dinners and is a remarkable resource for researchers, teachers, students, and history buffs.

ADDITIONAL RESOURCES BY CHAPTER

KEYSTONE STATE, ETERNAL CITY

Gettysburg sources appear in notes for Abraham Lincoln in the following pages.

PART I

CHAPTER 1

Information regarding the signers of the Declaration of Independence and early colonial history of the United States found here and in notes to chapter 4, on page 268, comes primarily from two books that I coauthored with my husband, Joseph D'Agnese: *Signing Their Lives Away: The Fame and Misfortune of the Men Who Signed the Declaration of Independence* (Philadelphia: Quirk Books, 2009) and *Signing Their Rights Away: The Fame and Misfortune of the Men Who Signed the United States*

Constitution (Philadelphia: Quirk Books, 2011). Hale's poem "Good Night" was included in *The School Song Book: Adapted to the Scenes of the School Room, Written for American Children and Youth* (Boston: Allen & Ticknor, 1834).

CHAPTER 2

I've lived in Rome twice in my life. Romulus and Remus are omnipresent— and also symbols for my favorite soccer team, A.S. Roma—and people like Cicero are quoted at dinner parties. For additional information on Cicero, see Spencer Cole, *Cicero and the Rise of Deification at Rome* (New York: Cambridge University Press, 2013). Numerous books, magazines, and reference materials describe ancient thanksgiving traditions. The book, edited by Robert Haven Schauffler, *Thanksgiving: Its Origin, Celebration and Significance as Related in Prose and Verse* (New York: Moffat, Yard, 1915) covers a lot of ground. For some additional harvest festival information, see: William Smith, ed., *A Dictionary of Greek and Roman Antiquities* (London: John Murray, 1875); A. Makris, "Thesmophoria: An Ancient Greek Thanksgiving Celebration," usa.GreekReporter.com, Nov. 21, 2012; Michael Gilligan, "Lughnasa Recipes, Rituals, Traditions and Symbols for the Ancient Celtic Festival," irishcentral.com, Aug. 1, 2019; Emmett McIntyre, "Celtic Harvest Festival of Lughnasa," transceltic.com, July 26, 2016; Janet Milhomme, "Ghanaians Hoot at Hunger. Ga Tribe Hosts Its Own Kind of Thanksgiving. African Harvesttime," *Christian Science Monitor*, Nov. 21, 1988; Evan Andrews, "5 Ancient New Year's Celebrations," history.com, Dec. 31, 2012; "The History of Thanksgiving and Its Celebrations," *Queens Gazette* (New York), Nov. 23, 2016; and "Makar Sankranti 2020: Date, Time and Shubh Muhurat," *Times of India*, Jan. 13, 2020.

The Codex Sinaiticus is fascinating to look into, and now anyone can, thanks to a joint effort from the British Library, National Library of Russia, St. Catherine's Monastery, and Leipzig University Library (www.codexsinaiticus.org). Bible history, including King James and Tyndale, is from *"Translation . . . openeth the window to let in the light": The Pre-History and Abiding Impact of the King James Bible*, a virtual exhibit at Ohio State University, Eric J. Johnson, curator.

The Spanish Armada thanksgiving is cited extensively, and again I like Schauffler's *Thanksgiving*. The Tudor Society and its magazine, *Tudor Life*, have several articles and videos as well. For a discussion of migratory patterns and genetic sampling, see Adam Rutherford, "A New History of the First Peoples in the Americas," *Atlantic*, Oct. 3, 2017. For early thanksgivings in North America, the Library of Congress has a "Thanks-

giving Timeline, 1541–2001" (https://loc.gov/teachers/classroommater
ials/presentationsandactivities/presentations/thanksgiving/timeline/1541
.html), which includes Coronado, the Huguenots, Popham, Jamestown,
and more. See also, Amanda Williamson, "Festival to Offer Remembrance
of Huguenots," *Florida Times-Union*, Sept. 24, 2015; for Coronado, see
Mike Kingston, "The First Thanksgiving," *Texas Almanac* (adapted from
his article and posted at https://texasalmanac.com/topics/history/time
line/first-thanksgiving); "Who Celebrated the 'First Thanksgiving'?" Library of Congress Wise Guide (https://www.loc.gov/wiseguide/nov02
/thanks-early.html). See the National Parks Service of St. Augustine, Florida, for documentation of that location's "First Thanksgiving"; Christine
Sismondo, "The Odd, Complicated History of Canadian Thanksgiving,"
Maclean's, Oct. 5, 2017; Myron Beckenstein, "Maine's Lost Colony," *Smithsonian Magazine*, Feb. 2004. Berkeley Plantation has many resources about
their historic site, including H. Graham Woodlief, "History of the First
Thanksgiving," Berkeley Plantation: Virginia's Most Historic Plantation
(http://www.berkeleyplantation.com/first-thanksgiving.html).

For the Haudenosaunee Thanksgiving Address and much more on the
Six Nations, see the "Haudenosaunee Guide for Educators," Education
Office, Smithsonian Institution's National Museum of the American Indian (https://americanindian.si.edu/sites/1/files/pdf/education/Haude
nosauneeGuide.pdf).

CHAPTER 3

See Hale sources in the Global Notes on page 263. For Lydia Maria
Child, here and in future chapters, see: Lydia Maria Child, *Hobomok and
Other Writings on Indians*, Carolyn L. Karcher, ed. (New Brunswick, NJ:
Rutgers University Press, 1986); *A Lydia Maria Child Reader*, Carolyn L.
Karcher, ed. (Durham, NC: Duke University Press, 1997); Carolyn L.
Karcher, *The First Woman in the Republic: A Cultural Biography of Lydia
Maria Child* (Durham, NC: Duke University Press, 1994).

There are countless articles that distinguish between general thanksgivings, feast days, and harvest festivals. A good book that does just that
is William DeLoss Love Jr.'s *The Fast and Thanksgiving Days of New
England* (Boston: Houghton, Mifflin, 1895).

Information regarding the Seminole Wars: https://seminolenation
museum.org. For David Hale's death, see "Sudden Death," *Plattsburgh
Republican*, May 4, 1839; Theo. F. Rodenbough and William L. Haskin,
eds., "The First Regiment of Artillery," in *The Army of the United States:
Historical Sketches of Staff and Line with Portraits of Generals-in-Chief*
(New York: Maynard, Merrill, 1896).

SELECTED NOTES AND SOURCES

CHAPTER 4

"Founders Online," hosted by the National Archives (https://founders
.archives.gov), is a fantastic clearinghouse of nearly 200,000 documents
by early American players, including George Washington, Thomas Jefferson, and John Adams.

For additional information on George Washington's inauguration
from George Washington's Mount Vernon, which also includes links to
their archives, see: "President-Elect George Washington's Journey to the
Inauguration" (http://www.mountvernon.org/george-washington/the
-first-president/inauguration).

The Massachusetts Historical Society is a wonderful resource for
many reasons, including access to the Adams Family Papers (http://
www.masshist.org/adams/adams-family-papers). Samuel Adams's proclamations are from newspaper accounts and Ira Stoll's *Samuel Adams: A
Life* (New York: Free Press, 2008); and *The Writings of Samuel Adams*,
vol. IV, *1778–1802*, Harry Alonzo Cushing, ed. (New York: G. P. Putnam's Sons, 1908). Details surrounding Washington's first thanksgiving
proclamation are also from the Mount Vernon website. Details of the day
and reception are from the Library of Congress, including "Thanksgiving
Timeline," "Today in History—November 26," the George Washington,
Papers at the Library of Congress; *The Diaries of George Washington*, 6
vols., Donald Jackson and Dorothy Twohig, eds. (Charlottesville: University Press of Virginia, 1976–79); and "The Washington Papers," an online
archive at the University of Virginia (https://washingtonpapers.org). On
Thomas Jefferson, see: "From Thomas Jefferson to Samuel Miller, 23
January 1808," Founders Online, National Archives (founders.archives
.gov/documents/Jefferson/99-01-02-7257). John Adams's reflection on
his declared fast is also available at Founders Online, as well as his papers.

CHAPTER 5

Food resources include: Alan Davidson, *The Oxford Companion to Food*
(Oxford: Oxford University Press, 1999); Judith A. Barter, ed., *Art and
Appetite: American Painting, Culture, and Cuisine* (Chicago: Art Institute
of Chicago, 2013); *Inside Adams: Science, Technology & Business* (Library
of Congress blog, ed. Ellen Terrell), "A Brief History of Pumpkin Pie in
America," by Alison Kelly, posted Nov. 20, 2017. Information on the
Seneca Falls Convention is widely available, and the Women's Rights
National Historical Park, managed by the National Park Service, is a fine
resource (https://www.nps.gov/wori/index.htm). Additional discussion
on the Panic of 1837 is from *Our Sister Editors* (Okker). "The New-
England Boy's Song About Thanksgiving" is from Lydia Maria Child,

Flowers for Children, II (New York: C. S. Francis, 1845). For presidential backgrounds, speeches, and other information, see Global Notes. Greenwood's firing, from National Woman Suffrage Association, *Report of the International Council of Women: Assembled by the National Woman Suffrage Association, Washington, D.C., U.S. of America, March 25 to April 1, 1888* (Washington, DC: Rufus H. Darby, Printer, 1888).

Hale's reissuing of *Northwood* and discussions of Liberia: Harriet Beecher Stowe, *Uncle Tom's Cabin or, Life Among the Lowly* (Boston: John P. Jewett, 1852); Frederick Douglass quote is from the *Frederick Douglass' Paper* 5, no. 5 (Jan. 22, 1852), retrieved from the Gates Collection of African American History and Culture, 1820–1998, at Portland State University; additional information on the American Colonization Society is also from the Gates Collection, as well as from Nicholas Guyatt, "The American Colonization Society: 200 Years of the 'Colonizing Trick,'" African American Intellectual History Society, Dec. 22, 2016; Susan Campbell, "Ending of Landmark Book, 'Uncle Tom's Cabin,' Is Still Debated," *Hartford Courant*, Feb. 16, 2014; for other present-day discussions of Stowe and Hale on the topic, see the Global Notes. Abraham Lincoln's speech of Oct. 16, 1854, is widely available, including at the Lincoln Home, National Historic Site, administered by the National Park Service.

I wish more of Amelia Bloomer could be in this book. Additional information, including Godey's reluctance to embrace the trend, is from Gayle V. Fischer, *Pantaloons and Power: A Nineteenth-Century Dress Reform in the United States* (Kent, OH: Kent State University Press, 2001); Carol Mattingly, *Appropriate[ing] Dress: Women's Rhetorical Style in Nineteenth-Century America* (Carbondale: Southern Illinois University Press, 2002).

PART II

Global notes for Civil War, Gettysburg, and Lincoln.

I have had the privilege of walking the grounds of both Fort Sumter and Gettysburg with knowledgeable historic guides. However, just being there on those grounds adds so very much. The amount of material available on Abraham Lincoln alone borders on unfathomable. Key sources that served my needs in Part II of this book include: Abraham Lincoln Papers at the Library of Congress (http://memory.loc.gov/ammem /alhtml/malhome.html); Harold Holzer, ed., *Dear Mr. Lincoln: Letters to the President* (Reading, MA: Addison-Wesley, 1993); Matthew Pinsker, *Lincoln's Sanctuary: Abraham Lincoln and the Soldiers' Home* (New York: Oxford University Press, 2003); Philip B. Kunhardt Jr., *A New Birth of*

Freedom: Lincoln at Gettysburg (Boston: Little, Brown, 1983); Tyler Dennett, ed., *Lincoln and the Civil War in the Diaries and Letters of John Hay* (New York: Dodd, Mead, 1939); "Civil War Timeline," Gettysburg National Military Park, PA; and National Portrait Gallery's "CivilWar@ Smithsonian" (http://civilwar.si.edu) has archival collections, photographs, timelines, and additional resources. The Abraham Lincoln Association published *The Collected Works of Abraham Lincoln* in 1953, and the University of Michigan has made them available online (https://quod.lib. umich.edu/l/lincoln). It is invaluable for research. Art and illustrations are key parts of this book, and Thomas Nast's work is mentioned throughout Part II. The illustrations have been scanned by university libraries and collectors, and in more scans of *Harper's Weekly*. The University of Pennsylvania (https://onlinebooks.library.upenn.edu/webbin /serial?id=harpersweekly) lists where scans of *Harper's Weekly* are available via the Internet Archive (http://archive.org); and HathiTrust has scans provided by the University of Chicago, the University of Michigan, and Pennsylvania State University (https://catalog.hathitrust.org/Record /000061498). See also Fiona Deans Halloran, *Thomas Nast: The Father of Modern Political Cartoons* (Chapel Hill: University of North Carolina Press, 2012).

ADDITIONAL RESOURCES BY CHAPTER

CHAPTER 6

More on Fort Sumter: Fergus M. Bordewich, "Fort Sumter: The Civil War Begins," *Smithsonian Magazine*, April 2011; Kee Malesky, "The Civil War's First Death Was an Accident," *NPR Weekend Edition Saturday* (transcript), April 9, 2011 (https://www.npr.org/2011/04/09/135247928 /the-civil-wars-first-death-was-an-accident); and the National Park Service site for Fort Sumter and Fort Moultrie, National Historical Park, SC (https://www.nps.gov/fosu/index.htm).

For Vassar information, see Global Notes to Part I. For North Carolina's 1849 thanksgiving: North Carolina Department of Natural and Cultural Resources, "Tracing the History of Thanksgiving in North Carolina," Nov. 25, 2015 (https://www.ncdcr.gov/blog/2015/11/25/tracing -the-history-of-thanksgiving-in-north-carolina); for Georgia, reported in the *United States Gazette* (Philadelphia), Dec. 29, 1826; Thomas Smyth, *The Battle of Fort Sumter: Its Mystery and Miracle: God's Mastery and Mercy. A Discourse Preached on the Day of National Fasting, Thanksgiving and Prayer, in the First Presbyterian Church, Charleston, S. C., June 13, 1861* (Charleston: Southern Guardian Steam-Power Press, 1861).

For the Lewis Hayden–John Albion Andrew thanksgiving dinner, and proposed 54th Regiment: "Lewis Hayden and the Underground Railroad," the Commonwealth Museum, online exhibit about Hayden's life (http://www.sec.state.ma.us/mus/pdfs/Lewis-Hayden.pdf); June Wulff, "Lasting Lessons in an 1862 Boston Thanksgiving," *Boston Globe*, Nov. 20, 2012; news brief, *The Liberator* (Boston), Jan. 23, 1863. Harriet Tubman and connection to Hunter: "Harriet Tubman's Great Raid," *New York Times*, June 7, 2013. Broadside and other information regarding recruitment of Black soldiers during the Civil War: "Black Soldiers in the U.S. Military During the Civil War," a collection of archival documents and resources at the National Archives (https://www.archives.gov/education/lessons/blacks-civil-war). This includes information on Frederick Douglass's sons. For Gooding: Corporal James Henry Gooding, *On the Altar of Freedom: A Black Soldier's Civil War Letters from the Front*, Virginia M. Adams, ed. (Amherst: University of Massachusetts Press, 1991).

And as for the letter Hale wrote to Lincoln: Abraham Lincoln Papers at the Library of Congress, Series 1, General Correspondence, 1833–1916. Sarah J. Hale to Abraham Lincoln, Monday, September 28, 1863 (https://memory.loc.gov/cgi-bin/ampage?collId=mal&fileName=mal1/266/2669900/malpage.db&recNum=0).

CHAPTER 7

Seward and Lincoln dialogue from Frederick W. Seward, *Seward at Washington as Senator and Secretary of State: A Memoir of His Life, with Selections from His Letters, 1861–1872* (New York: Derby and Miller, 1891). "The President's Emancipation March," George E. Fawcett, available at the Library of Congress. For proclamations, see Global Notes. For sheet music to the president's hymn, see the Library of Congress at https://www.loc.gov/item/scsm000143; the hymn was published: William Augustus Muhlenberg, "The President's Hymn: Give Thanks All Ye People, in Response to the Proclamation of the President of the United States Recommending a General Thanksgiving on November 26th, 1863" (New York: A. D. F. Randolph, 1864); news of hymn appeared on thanksgiving day, 1863: "The President's Hymn," *Chicago Tribune*, Nov. 26, 1863. *Ironsides*: "From Washington," *Chicago Tribune*, Oct. 15, 1863, and "The Torpedo Trial in Charleston Harbor—Further Particulars," *Richmond Dispatch* (VA), Oct. 12, 1863. Emerson quote is from *The Complete Works of Ralph Waldo Emerson*, vol. 11, *Miscellanies* (Boston: Houghton Mifflin, 1883); available online at https://www.rwe.org.

CHAPTER 8

For Uncle Sam background, see: *O Say Can You See?: Stories from the Museum* (blog of National Museum of American History, Smithsonian

SELECTED NOTES AND SOURCES

Institution), "Uncle Sam: The Man and the Meme," by Natalie Elder, posted Sept. 13, 2013. Washington's letter to Wheatley in the George Washington Papers Series 3 (see Chapter 4 notes). See also Anne Holmes, "Phillis Wheatley: A First for Verse in America," *LCM*, the Library of Congress Magazine, Jan./Feb. 2018 (https://blogs.loc.gov/catbird/2018/01/phillis-wheatley-a-first-for-verse-in-america). "Hard Tack": Wayne Phaneuf, "Civil War, November 1863: Gettysburg Address, First National Thanksgiving, Local Boys Are Heroes," MassLive.com, Nov. 3, 2013. Barton: "Thanksgiving & the Civil War," Clara Barton Missing Soldiers Office Museum, Nov. 27, 2014 (https://www.clarabarton museum.org/thanksgiving-the-civil-war). Fort Wagner: "Fort Wagner, Battery Wagner, Morris Island," American Battlefield Trust. ABT is a terrific repository of maps, primary sources, and more (http://www.battlefields.org/learn/civil-war/battles/fort-wagner). The Library of Congress also has 1863 maps of this area and others available online (www.loc.gov/collections/civil-war-maps). Fascinating stuff. Lewis Douglass to Amelia: Pamela Newkirk, ed., *Letters from Black America* (New York: Farrar, Straus and Giroux, 2009). "Tickled diaphragms": "From General Gillmore's Army," *New South* (Port Royal, SC), Nov. 28, 1863. Woodlin: "Woodlin, William P. (fl. 1863–1864) [Diary of an African American soldier in 8th Regiment United States Colored Troops, Company G]," Gilder Lehrman Institute of American History. Sojourner Truth: Nell Irvin Painter, *Sojourner Truth: A Life a Symbol* (New York: W. W. Norton, 1996); Sojourner Truth, Olive Gilbert, and Frances W. Titus, *Narrative of Sojourner Truth* (Battle Creek, MI: Review and Herald Office, 1884); and Sojourner Truth Institute of Battle Creek (https://sojournertruth.org). References to charity, celebrations, balls, church services, etc. come from dozens of newspaper accounts (retrieved via, primarily, Chronicling America at loc.gov and from newspapers.com), including: Thanksgiving Ball: *Placer Herald* (Rocklin, CA), Nov. 28, 1863; Missouri proclamation: *Weekly Herald and Tribune* (St. Joseph, MO), Nov. 26, 1863; Wheeling Soldier's Fund: *Wheeling Daily Intelligencer* (WV), Nov. 25, 1863; "Let Us Give Thanks!" *Advocate* (Buffalo, NY), Nov. 26, 1863; "Convalescent Camp," *Nashville Daily Union* (TN), Nov. 29, 1863; Meridian Hill House, *Evening Star* (Washington, DC), Nov. 25, 1863; Charleston Proclamation: *Charleston Mercury*, Nov. 13, 1863; "A Festive Day," *Daily True Delta* (New Orleans), Nov. 27, 1863; *New South* (Port Royal, SC), Nov. 28, 1863; Washington Proclamation in *Washington Standard*, Nov. 21, 1863; "Thanksgiving Notice," *Pacific Commercial Advertiser* (Honolulu), Nov. 19, 1863; "London Times on Lincoln's Thanksgiving Proclamation," *Weekly Advertiser* (Montgomery, AL), Nov. 25, 1863; Kansas observance: *Leavenworth Bulletin*

(KS), Nov. 25, 1863; California Proclamation: *Sonoma County Journal* (Petaluma, CA), Nov. 27, 1863; ad selection, foods: *Evening Star* (Washington, DC), Nov. 25, 1863; Dow & Burkhardt's ad: *Louisville Daily Journal* (KY), Nov. 16, 1863; "Greedy Thief," *Santa Cruz Weekly Sentinel* (CA), Nov. 26, 1863; Thanksgiving in Berlin: *New York Times*, Dec. 27, 1863; "Ford's New Theater": *Evening Star* (Washington, DC), Nov. 25, 1863.

CHAPTER 9

Gilbert King, "The History of Pardoning Turkeys Began with Tad Lincoln," *Smithsonian Magazine*, Nov. 21, 2012. Walt Whitman, *Complete Prose Works* (Philadelphia: David McKay, 1892) and *Leaves of Grass*, 4th ed. (New York: William E. Chapin, 1867); the Walt Whitman Archive and Project Gutenberg, among others, have made these available online. Lincoln shot at: Carl Sandburg, *Abraham Lincoln: The War Years* (New York: Harcourt, Brace, 1936) and Don E. Fehrenbacher and Virginia Fehrenbacher, eds., *Recollected Words of Abraham Lincoln* (Stanford, CA: Stanford University Press, 1996). Robert Todd Lincoln information widely available, including at UVA's Miller Center (see Global Notes). Hale to Seward from *The Collected Works of Abraham Lincoln*, vol. 8. Newspaper reports of thanksgiving celebrations—*Chicago Tribune, Nashville Union, New York Herald, Gold Hill Daily News* (Gold Hill, NV), etc. include: multiple articles, *Chicago Tribune*, Nov. 23 and Nov. 24, 1863; *Nashville Daily Union*, Nov. 24, 1864; "Our National Thanksgiving," *New York Daily Herald*, Nov. 25, 1864; "The Thanksgiving Dinner of the Newsboys," *Brooklyn Union*, Nov. 25, 1864; "Thanksgiving Day," *Evening Star* (Washington, DC), Nov. 25, 1864; "Thanksgiving Dinner," *Gold Hill Daily News*, Nov. 23, 1864; Turkeys for Lee's boys: "Items," *Yorkville Enquirer* (York, SC), Nov. 15, 1864; "The War News," *Richmond Daily Dispatch*, Nov. 25, 1864; "From Petersburg," *Yorkville Enquirer* (York, SC), Nov. 30, 1864.

CHAPTER 10

The New York Public Library's Manuscripts and Archives Division is one of my favorite places on planet, and the archivists there are spectacular. Their collection of U.S. Sanitary Commission records boggles the mind and is a unique way to look at the Civil War. I did much research into the commission, initially thinking the organization and Elizabeth Blackwell might play a much larger role in the story. Some other time . . . One of the U.S. Sanitary Commission's physicians was Charles A. Leale. As the first doctor to reach Abraham Lincoln after he was shot, Leale's personal account of that evening is a compelling read. Visit the National Archives to read it yourself in Leale's own handwriting: "Report of Assistant Surgeon Charles A. Leale Concerning the Death of Abraham Lincoln," Records of the Adjutant General's Office, 1762–1984, Special Files, 1790–1946, Special File #14: Medical Records File on President Lincoln's Assassination containing File "D"-776-Medical File, and Items A–B. See also Helena Iles Papaioannou and Daniel W. Stowell, "Dr. Charles A. Leale's Report on the Assassination of Abraham Lincoln," *Journal of the Abraham Lincoln Association* 34, no. 1 (Winter 2013): 40–53; Ray Cavanaugh, "Our American Cousin: Lincoln's Fateful Night at the Theatre," *Guardian*, April 6, 2015. See also Seward's memoir, previously cited in notes to chapter 7. Native peoples in the Civil War: "We Are All Americans," City of Alexandria, VA (alexandriava.gov/historic/fortward). Grant and Parker: "Ely S. Parker Building Officially Opens," U.S. Dept. of the Interior, Dec. 21, 2000 (https://www.bia.gov) and Mary Stockwell, "Ulysses Grant's Failed Attempt to Grant Native Americans Citizenship," *Smithsonian Magazine*, Jan. 9, 2019. Lincoln's final speech, more on evening of assassination: Henry Louis Gates Jr. with David W. Blight and Neal Conan, "Scholar Reappraises President Lincoln" (transcript), *Talk of the Nation*, National Public Radio, Feb. 11, 2009; "Andrew Johnson, 16th Vice President (1865)" (https://www.senate.gov/about/officers-staff/vice -president/VP_Andrew_Johnson.htm); David S. Reynolds, "John Wilkes Booth and the Higher Law," *Atlantic*, April 12, 2015; Doris Kearns Goodwin, *Team of Rivals: The Political Genius of Abraham Lincoln* (New York: Simon & Schuster, 2005); *Constitution Daily* (blog), "The Forgotten Man Who Almost Became President after Lincoln" (https://constitutioncenter .org); "Andrew Johnson," Miller Center of Public Affairs, University of Virginia (https://millercenter.org/president/johnson); "The Swearing In of Andrew Johnson," Joint Congressional Committee on Inaugural Ceremonies (https://www.inaugural.senate.gov/about/past-inaugural-ceremonies /swearing-in-of-vice-president-andrew-johnson-after-the-assassination-of -president-abraham-lincoln/index.html); *Constitution Daily* (blog), "When Presidential Inaugurations Go Very, Very Wrong," by Scott Bomboy, posted Jan. 18, 2017; Mahita Gajanan, "These Are the Bible Verses Past Presidents Have Turned to on Inauguration Day," *Time*, Jan. 19, 2017. Threats: *Dear Mr. Lincoln*, see Global Notes to Part II, on page 269. Walt Whitman, see notes to Chapter 9. Douglass walking stick: Frederick Douglass National Historic Site, National Park Service; Papers and Images of the American Civil War, Collection Reference GLC02474, Gilder Lehrman Institute of American History. Newspaper accounts of celebration of the holiday retrieved from newspapers.com. Grant and Parker as previously cited.

PART III

CHAPTER 11

Grant final speech, Twain and Hayes: UVA Miller Center (see Global Notes). Hale as cited in Global Notes. Sale of *Godey's*: "Interesting Collection Tidbits: Godey's Magazine and Lady's Book," State Library of Pennsylvania (https://www.statelibrary.pa.gov/Pages/Rare-Collections -Spotlight.aspx); Beverly C. Tomek, "Godey's Lady's Book," *The Encyclopedia of Greater Philadelphia* (https://philadelphiaencyclopedia.org /archive/godeys-ladys-book). Obituaries, tributes: "Death of Mrs. Sarah J. Hale," *Wisconsin State Journal* (Madison), May 1, 1879; "Louis A. Godey," *Times* (Philadelphia), Nov. 31, 1878; "A Noted Woman: Incidents of the Life of Mrs. Hale, the Venerable Authoress," *St. Joseph Gazette-Herald* (MO), May 9, 1879; "Sarah Josepha Buell Hale," *Philadelphia Inquirer*, May 1, 1879; "Mrs. Sarah J. Hale," *Granite Monthly* III, Oct. 1879. Cherokee proclamations: "Indian Thanksgiving: A Cherokee Chief's Proclamation," *Latter-Day Saints' Millennial Star* XLV, Jan. 15, 1883; "An Indian Chief's Thanksgiving Proclamation," *Council Fire and Arbitrator* VII, Dec. 1884; Melissa Howell, "Cherokees' 1885 Thanksgiving Proclamation Draws Questions," *Oklahoman*, Nov. 28, 2013; Mayes 1891 proclamation from DeLoss Love, *The Fast and Thanksgiving Days of New England*, cited in notes to chapter 3.

CHAPTER 12

Football: Neil Reynolds, "Why Do We Play on Thanksgiving Day?," NFL .com, Nov. 24, 2019; Dombonvissuto, "1920 Akron Pros Fob," History of the NFL in 95 Objects, *Sports Illustrated*, June 10, 2014; evolving thanksgiving celebrations: page 46, multiple articles (multicultural, vegetarian, etc.), *Chicago Tribune*, Nov. 21, 1897; "Thanksgiving Day," *New Education* XI, Nov. 1898; Knoxville as cited in text; Hooverizing: "Hooverize on Thanksgiving; Here's Menu," *Santa Barbara Daily News and the Independent*, Nov. 22, 1917; *The History Kitchen* (PBS blog), "Discover the History of Meatless Mondays," by Tori Avey, posted Aug. 16, 2013; "Thanksgiving Dinner Appeal," *New York Times*, Nov. 6, 1918; Gena Philibert-Ortega, "Rationing Thanksgiving Dinner During World War I," Nov. 27, 2013 (https://blog.genealogybank.com/rationing-thanksgiving -dinner-during-world-war-i.html). Armistice: George H. McKnight, "For a Day of Thanksgiving," letter to *New York Times*, Nov. 20, 1918.

The Spanish flu began to take on a whole new level of meaning during the era of COVID-19. The University of Michigan Center for the History of Medicine and Michigan Publishing, University of Michigan Library, has compiled a remarkable database, the American Influenza Epidemic of 1918–1919: A Digital Encyclopedia (https://www.influenzaarchive .org). See also: Kevin Dayhoff, "Government Censorship Made the 1918 Spanish Flu Even Worse," *Carroll County Times* (MD), Mar. 20, 2020; Gillian Brockell, "Trump Is Ignoring the Lessons of 1918 Flu Pandemic That Killed Millions, Historian Says," *Washington Post*, Feb. 29, 2020; "Thanksgiving Day Impressively Observed," *Deseret Evening Star* (Salt Lake City, UT), Nov. 28, 1918; "Santa Claus Is Down with the Flu," *St. Paul Daily News* (MN), Dec. 6, 1918; "Asks Thanksgiving Plans Be Restricted," *World-Herald* (Omaha), Nov. 28, 1918; "Only 83 Cases of Spanish Flu Thanksgiving," *Quad-City Times* (Davenport, IA), Nov. 28, 1918; "A Solemn Day Overseas," *Kansas City Star*, Nov. 28, 1918. I found a wonderful poem printed in *The Carolina Mountaineer and Waynesville Courier*, titled "The Spanish Flu May Get You, Too," by Jesse Daniel Boone. I couldn't use it. But look it up. It is a keeper. "A Thanksgiving Nuisance," *New York Times*, Nov. 30, 1918; Masking: "Thanksgiving," *New York Times*, Nov. 29, 1895; *Protojournalist* (National Public Radio blog), "When Thanksgiving Was Weird," by Linton Weeks, posted Nov. 23, 2014; Megan Garber, "Thanksgiving Used to Look a Lot Like Halloween, Except More Racist," *Atlantic*, Nov. 26, 2014.

Gimbel's and Macy's: Gimbel toy store ads: *Morning News* (Wilmington, DE), Nov. 13, 1920; *Philadelphia Inquirer*, Nov. 15, 1920; "The Toyland of Oz—Gimbel's," *Evening Public Ledger* (Philadelphia), Nov. 5, 1920; *PhillyHistory* (blog), "Floats, Balloons, and Celebrities, Oh My!: Philadelphia's Thanksgiving Day Parade," by Timothy Horning and Hillary Kativa, posted Nov. 22, 2010; Tommy Rowan, "Is Philly's Thanksgiving Day Parade Really the Oldest in America?," *Philadelphia Inquirer*, Nov. 22, 2017; Marielle Mondon, "The Wonderful—and Occasionally Weird—Philly Thanksgiving Day Parade Captured in Old Photos," *Philly Voice*, Nov. 21, 2017; Jerry Jonas, "Remembering Philly's Once Great Thanksgiving Day Parade," *Bucks County Courier Times* (PA), Nov. 22, 2015; Phil Luciano, "Saint Nick Has Been Parading in Peoria for Over a Century," *Journal Star* (Peoria, IL), Nov. 26, 2014; Vicki Cox, "Comin' to Town," *Chicago Tribune*, Nov. 21, 2004; Vicki Cox, "America's Longest-Running Christmas Parade," *American Profile*, Nov. 13, 2012; "At 100 Years, Philly Hosts Nation's Oldest Thanksgiving Day Parade," *WHYY* (PBS NPR), Nov. 28, 2019; Claire Suddath, "A Brief History of Macy's Thanksgiving Day Parade," *Time*, Nov. 27, 2008; "First Big NYC Thanksgiving Parade Had Zoo Animals," CBS Miami, Nov. 27, 2014.

CHAPTER 13

Harding, Coolidge: "President Harding Installed a Radio in the White House, February 8, 1922," America's Story (http://www. americaslibrary

.gov); Fireside Chats, Warm Springs: Presidency Project (see Global Notes); "Roosevelt's Little White House, State Historic Site, Warm Springs," Georgia State Parks & Historic Sites (http://www. gastateparks .org). World's Fair: Orrin E. Dunlap Jr., "Ceremony Is Carried by Television as Industry Makes Its Formal Bow," *New York Times*, May 1, 1939; Bruce Robertson, "Television at Fair Impresses Public," *Broadcasting*, May 15, 1939; Alan Taylor, "The 1939 New York World's Fair," *Atlantic*, Nov. 1, 2013.

Roosevelt, and the kerfuffle surrounding his changing the date of thanksgiving: G. Wallace Chessman, "Thanksgiving: Another FDR Experiment," *Prologue*, Fall 1990; additional letters and documentation: "The Year We Had Two Thanksgivings," Franklin D. Roosevelt Presidential Library and Museum (http://docs.fdrlibrary.marist.edu/thanksg .html); "Thanksgiving," *Eagle* (Bryan, TX), Nov. 30, 1939; "Thanksgiving Day Mixup Has Extended Right into Roosevelt's Own Family," *Fort Worth Star-Telegram*, Nov. 22, 1939.

Art and illustrations informed much of the book, and the art of Norman Rockwell and J. C. Leyendecker as seen on covers of the *Saturday Evening Post* are a delight to peruse. In addition to browsing the thanksgiving archives at the *Saturday Evening Post* (http://www.saturday eveningpost.com/collections/thanksgiving), books I enjoyed include: Laurence S. Cutler, Judy Goffman Cutler, and the National Museum of American Illustration, *J. C. Leyendecker: American Imagist* (New York: Abrams, 2008); Laura Claridge, *Norman Rockwell: A Life* (New York: Random House, 2001); Norman Rockwell, *My Adventures as an Illustrator* (Indianapolis: Curtis, 1979).

Pilgrims, Puritans, Native peoples: For a deep dive into the story of the Wampanoag and their interactions with the Pilgrims and Puritans: David J. Silverman, *This Land Is Their Land: The Wampanoag Indians, Plymouth Colony, and the Troubled History of Thanksgiving* (New York: Bloomsbury, 2019). Additional sources on the topic of the mythical "first" thanksgiving include (but are definitely not limited to): Robert Tracy McKenzie, *The First Thanksgiving: What the Real Story Tells Us About Loving God and Learning from History* (Downers Grove, IL: IVP Academic, 2013). "Thanksgiving in North America," an online collection of resources from the Smithsonian Institution (https://www.si.edu/spot light/thanksgiving), has art, menus, food history, Native American perspectives, and educational resources; Pilgrim Hall Museum (https:// pilgrimhall.org/thanksgiving.htm) has an extensive thanksgiving collection, including primary sources, and is a good place for newcomers to the story to start. There you can find texts from *Mourt's Relation*, by Edward Winslow, as well as *Of Plimoth Plantation*, by William Bradford, the only existing references to the events of 1621. In 1841, Alexander Young published an anthology, *Chronicles of the Pilgrim Fathers of the Colony of Plymouth, from 1602 to 1625* (Boston: Charles C. Little and James Brown), which included *Mourt's Relation*. On page 231, he footnoted this account as: "This was the first Thanksgiving, the harvest festival of New England."

Additional information about the myth building, including in magazines: The J. H. A. Bone article "The First New England Thanksgiving" was a treat to find. It was printed very widely but first appeared in *Our Young Folks, an Illustrated Magazine for Boys and Girls* V, Nov. 1869; H. Maria George, "The Story of Thanksgiving Day," *Demorest's Monthly Magazine* XXIV, Nov. 1887–Oct. 1888; "Thanksgiving, 1775–1875," *New York Times*, Nov. 25, 1875; "A National Thanksgiving," *New York Times*, Nov. 23, 1890. Turkey: *Oxford Companion to Food*, see notes to chapter 5, and *Cool Green Science* (Nature Conservancy blog), "Tracing the Wild Origins of the Domestic Turkey," by Joe Smith, posted Nov. 20, 2017. Jane G. Austin, *Standish of Standish: A Story of the Pilgrims* (Boston: Houghton, Mifflin, 1889); Clifford Howard, "The First Thanksgiving Dinner," *Ladies' Home Journal*, Nov. 1897, 3–4; "Thanksgiving References," *Journal of Education* 50, no. 17 (Nov. 2, 1899); Andrew F. Smith, "The First Thanksgiving," *Gastronomica: The Journal for Food Studies* 3, no. 4 (Fall 2003): 79–85; DeLoss Love, *The Fast and Thanksgiving Days of New England*, cited in notes to chapter 3.

Additional information regarding congressional establishment of Thanksgiving (besides *Prologue*, previously cited) can be found at the National Archives, and includes scans of the resolutions: "Congress Establishes Thanksgiving" (https://www.archives.gov/legislative/features/thanksgiving). Macy's cancellation: History of the parade available on macys.com. Also: Christina Caron, "Macy's Used to Set the Balloons Free, and Other Thanksgiving Day Parade Facts," *New York Times*, Nov. 22, 2017. Rockwell as cited previously on page 277. Carlos Bulosan, "Freedom from Want," *Saturday Evening Post*, Mar. 6, 1943. Dick Hagelberg: "Thanksgiving Archives," *Saturday Evening Post* (www.saturdayeveningpost.com/collections/thanksgiving) and "A Rockwell Mother's Day," *Saturday Evening Post*, May 4, 2016.

CHAPTER 14

1972 protest: "Indians Protest at Site of First Thanksgiving," *El Dorado Times* (El Dorado, AR), Nov. 24, 1972; "Indians Bury Plymouth Rock," *Fresno Bee*, Nov. 27, 1970. Flag over Capitol and 1973 event: Paul J. Deveney, "Pilgrim Descendants Give Thanks to Massasoit," *Boston Globe*, Nov. 25, 1973. 1959: *Texas Almanac*, see notes to Chapter 2. John F.

Kennedy: James W. Baker, *Thanksgiving: The Biography of an American Holiday* (Lebanon: University of New Hampshire Press, 2009). Edward Kennedy report, *Indian Education: A National Tragedy—A National Challenge, 1969 Report of the Committee on Labor and Public Welfare, United States Senate Made by Its Special Subcommittee on Indian Education Pursuant to S. Res. 80*, National Indian Law Library (http://narf.org/nill /resources/education/reports/kennedy/toc.html). Dedication of Massasoit statue: "Red Men Dedicate Plymouth Statue," *Boston Globe*, Sept. 14, 1922; "Red Men to Hold 75th Great Sun Council Fire in Boston," *Boston Globe*, Sept. 8, 1922; J. R. Milne, "Descendant of Massasoit 'the Friend of the Pilgrims' Toils in Fields for Living," *Boston Post*, Aug. 15, 1920; Lisa Blee and Jean M. O'Brien, *Monumental Mobility: The Memory Work of Massasoit* (Chapel Hill: University of North Carolina Press, 2019). Macy's Pilgrims from their website (https://macysthanksgiving.fandom .com/wiki/The_50th_Annual_Macy%27s_Thanksgiving_Day_Parade_ Lineup). Proclamations as cited in Global Notes. Franklin on Iroquois, and "Iroquois Constitution: A Forerunner to Colonists' Democratic Principles," *New York Times*, June 28, 1987; Cynthia Feathers and Susan Feathers, "Franklin and the Iroquois Foundations of the Constitution," *Pennsylvania Gazette*, Jan./Feb. 2007; thirteen arrows: "Influence on Democracy," Official Website of the Haudenosaunee Confederacy (www.haudenosauneeco nfederacy.com/influence-on-democracy); Smithsonian Institution's "Haudenosaunee Guide for Educators," see notes to Chapter 2. Obama, Every Student Succeeds Act: "ESSA and Native American, Alaska Native, and Native Hawai'ian Students," Policy Center of the American Institutes for Research (https://www.air.org/resource/essa-and-native-american -alaska-native-and-native-hawaiian-students). Repatriation information provided by the Repatriation Office, National Museum of the American Indian, Smithsonian Institution; Jason Daley, "Massasoit, Chief Who Signed Treaty with the Pilgrims, to Be Reburied," *Smithsonian Magazine*, April 21, 2017. U.S. Mint: "Native American $1 Coin: 2011 Wampanoag Treaty of 1621" (https://www.usmint.gov/learn/kids/library/native -american-dollar-coins/2011-wampanoag-treaty-1621). M. F. K. Fisher: Christine VanDeVelde, "For Writer M. F. K. Fisher, Dining Properly Is an Art," *Los Angeles Times*, Nov. 24, 1989; M. F. K. Fisher, *The Gastronomical Me* (New York: Duell, Sloan & Pearce, 1943).

CHAPTER 15

Marble Collegiate Church history and information about Dr. Arthur Caliandro is from Marble Collegiate Church (https://www.marblechurch .org/welcome/history). The amount of information available regarding the benefits of gratitude is compelling, overwhelming, and inspirational.

Health benefits—mental and physical—are widely documented. Good places to start are: Christina Karns, "New Thoughts about Gratitude, Charity and Our Brains," *Washington Post*, Dec. 23, 2018; "In Praise of Gratitude," *Harvard Mental Health Letter*, June 5, 2019; Amy Morin, "7 Scientifically Proven Benefits of Gratitude," *Psychology Today*, April 3, 2015; Robert A. Emmons and Michael E. McCullough, "Counting Blessings Versus Burdens: An Experimental Investigation of Gratitude and Subjective Well-being in Daily Life," *Journal of Personality and Social Psychology* 84, no. 2 (March 2003); Randy A. Sansone and Lori A. Sansone, "Gratitude and Well-being: The Benefits of Appreciation," *Psychiatry* 7, no. 11 (Nov. 2010); University of Oregon, "Journaling Inspires Altruism Through an Attitude of Gratitude," *ScienceDaily*, Dec. 14, 2017; Jeffrey J. Froh, William J. Sefick, and Robert A. Emmons, "Counting Blessings in Early Adolescents: An Experimental Study of Gratitude and Subjective Well-being," *Journal of School Psychology* 46, no. 2 (April 2008); Joel Wong and Joshua Brown, "How Gratitude Changes You and Your Brain," *Greater Good Magazine*, June 6, 2017; Robert Emmons, "How Gratitude Can Help You Through Hard Times," *Greater Good Magazine*, May 13, 2013; Summer Allen, "The Science of Gratitude," a white paper prepared for the John Templeton Foundation by the Greater Good Science Center at UC Berkeley, May 2018.

EPILOGUE

My experience roasting oysters in November 2018 was a fantastic one, and one I will write about in greater length and detail in a forthcoming book. Pope Francis: "Pope Francis' Three Christmas Ingredients: Joy, Prayer, Gratitude," *Catholic News Agency*, Dec. 17, 2017; "Pope Francis' Homily at St. Patrick's Cathedral," *New York Times*, Sept. 24, 2015; "First Vespers on the Solemnity of Mary, Mother of God, and Te Deum in Thanksgiving for the Past Year: Homily of His Holiness Pope Francis," Dec. 31, 2019. The Holy See makes all homilies available on its website: www.vatican.va; Sylvia Poggioli, "Pope Francis Delivers Special Prayer for End to Coronavirus Pandemic," *National Public Radio*, Mar. 27, 2020. Andrés: Sean Gregory, "'Without Empathy, Nothing Works.' Chef José Andrés Wants to Feed the World Through the Pandemic," *Time*, Mar. 26, 2020. Moore: Jennifer Hassan, "99-Year-Old Veteran Raises $33 Million for Britain's Health-Care System by Walking His Garden," *Washington Post*, April 20, 2020.

INDEX

INDEX

INDEX

INDEX

INDEX

INDEX

INDEX

INDEX

INDEX

ABOUT THE AUTHOR

Denise Kiernan is an author, journalist, and producer. Her last two books—*The Last Castle* and *The Girls of Atomic City*—were both instant *New York Times* bestsellers in both hardcover and paperback. *The Last Castle* was a *Wall Street Journal* bestseller, a finalist for the 2018 Thomas Wolfe Memorial Literary Award, and a finalist for the Southern Book Prize. *The Girls of Atomic City* was a *Los Angeles Times* and NPR bestseller, was named one of Amazon's Top 100 Best Books of 2013, and has been published in multiple languages. Kiernan has been a featured guest on many radio and television shows, including NPR's *Weekend Edition*, *PBS NewsHour*, MSNBC's *Morning Joe*, and *The Daily Show with Jon Stewart*.